CLASSIC PLANTING

CLASSIC PLANTING

FEATURING THE GARDENS OF BETH CHATTO,
CHRISTOPHER LLOYD, ROSEMARY VEREY,
PENELOPE HOBHOUSE AND MANY OTHERS

GEORGE PLUMPTRE
PHOTOGRAPHS BY TONY LORD

WARD LOCK

For my wife, Rara, who encouraged me to
write another book after a long gap, and
whose help brought it to happy fruition.

A WARD LOCK BOOK
First published in the UK 1998
by Ward Lock
Wellington House
125 Strand
London WC2R 0BB

A Cassell imprint

Distributed in the United States
by Sterling Publishing Co. Inc.
387 Park Avenue South
New York, NY 10016–8810

A British Library Cataloguing in Publication Data block
for this book may be obtained from the British Library

Edited by Caroline Ball
Designed by Harry Green

ISBN 0-7063-7722-2
Printed and bound in Spain by Bookprint SL, Barcelona

PAGE 1: Diascias and forget-me-nots create a subtly
coloured tapestry among the multi-hued leaves of
Salvia officinalis 'Tricolor'.

PAGE 2: Careful colour planning is a hallmark
of the planting at Sticky Wicket, Dorset.

RIGHT: Bringing early summer colour to a shady
corner are *Geranium sylvaticum* 'Mayflower' and
Viola cornuta 'Rosea'.

CONTENTS

INTRODUCTION

One lesson of contemporary planting is the priority given to foliage and form in addition to seasonal flowers, and the value of their combination in groups.

The title *Classic Planting* may give an impression of being somewhat presumptuous, that everything in the book claims a universal seal of approval. At the same time it suggests an air of establishment, of a style of gardening that has gained its reputation from years of admiration. In a sense, the book turns the subject on its head to reveal the many *different* ways that classic quality has been achieved by outstanding contemporary gardeners.

Plants are like people; not only should they be considered and assessed for their individual qualities, but equally importantly for their contribution to a group. It is its satisfaction as a neighbour, its part in the creation of schemes in different seasons and varying situations that determine the true success of any plant within a garden. And surely, as I hope each chapter reveals, it is the quest to achieve successful plant combinations that is the most rewarding aspect of gardening today. It is a point constantly remade by the figures whose gardens most often feature in the book: Beth Chatto, Penelope Hobhouse, Christopher Lloyd and Rosemary Verey. Christopher Lloyd summed up the situation when he said to me: 'People too often think of the plants, not the scene.' It is the elevation of a plant by its associated scene — whether on a miniature scale in a container or on a larger scale in a border, planted for a special time of the year or for particular conditions — and how this scene is achieved, that is an important thread running through *Classic Planting*.

Most of the gardeners will be familiar to readers, either through their writing or their gardens, and the intention of *Classic Planting* is to describe and compare their work in close detail, revealing many of the secrets behind their success. Beth Chatto began her garden, in demanding circumstances close to the Essex coast, some three decades ago. Her gardening style is closely

linked to her interest in plant ecology and for many years she has been recognized as being in the vanguard of contemporary gardening, especially with her creation of informal plant landscapes such as her now highly regarded gravel garden.

Quite different in background is Christopher Lloyd's garden in the south-east corner of England. Great Dixter is an inheritance from his gardening parents, who were influenced by their friend, Edwin Lutyens. His development of the garden and introduction of a masterly tapestry of plant combinations balance an awareness of the garden's past with his own skills as a plantsman and constant inquisitive interest in the plants he grows.

At Barnsley House, in the Cotswolds, Rosemary Verey had an existing garden framework but, in a manner comparable to Beth Chatto, has carried through the evolution of her garden over nearly four decades. During that time her growing experience and knowledge has manifested itself in subtle changes in the garden's planting, within an overall picture that well demonstrates how many different strands of gardening can be drawn together in a medium-sized garden.

Penelope Hobhouse established a seminal reputation as a plantswoman at Tintinhull, at the same time (like Beth Chatto, Christopher Lloyd and Rosemary Verey) reaching a wider audience as a garden writer. The garden of this seventeenth-century Somerset manor house, created by Phyllis Reiss half a century ago, has clear connections with the 'garden room' style of Hidcote and Sissinghurst, and one fascinating aspect of Penelope Hobhouse's work is to see how she developed plant combinations and arrangements that are sympathetic to the past yet contemporary in the style and choice of individual plants. Her experience and preferences are now being interpreted in her own new garden at Bettiscombe in Dorset.

This view across Beth Chatto's gravel garden reveals the seemingly informal drift-style of planting, with groups such as bright-flowered diascias in the foreground punctuated by vertical statements such as yellow verbascums and mauve alliums.

These are not the only gardeners whose experience contributes to this book. Pam Lewis has established at Sticky Wicket in Dorset outstanding planting schemes that are firmly based on her view of her garden as a self-supporting ecological unit. The garden also gives a remarkable demonstration of how the idea of colour-scheming plants, often regarded as rather out of date and unfashionable, can succeed in a contemporary style. At Eastgrove Cottage in Worcestershire, Carol and Malcolm Skinner have created a cottage garden that remains true to its traditions at the same time as being filled with bold planting, while the impact of Paul Williams's planting ideas on Bourton House in the Cotswolds prove that a traditional country house garden can be transformed in appearance without destroying the underlying air of establishment.

ABOVE Colour combinations are most effective when they are striking from a distance and also work on the small scale at close quarters, as shown above by this late-spring group.

RIGHT Massed planting of perennials, such as this spreading group of mixed knautias at Sticky Wicket, and the use of perennial grasses to provide background height are both integral features of contemporary planting.

LEFT Many of today's gardeners advocate a sense of adventure in their planting, with the bold use of both foliage and bright flower colours, none more so than Christopher Lloyd in parts of his garden at Great Dixter.

RIGHT This detail of the potager in Rosemary Verey's garden at Barnsley is an excellent illustration of the incorporation of flowers among the formally arranged vegetables.

Roy Strong, perhaps more than any other single gardener and garden writer, not least through writing about his own garden in Herefordshire, champions formality in the contemporary garden, and describes how it can be easily and effectively achieved in a garden of any size. The views of Robin Lane Fox, Oxford don and gardening correspondent of the *Financial Times*, have earned him a devoted following: he constantly stresses that today's gardening is primarily about understanding your plants, knowing their habits, choosing and grouping them with care, and not being afraid to be unconventional.

Other gardens are included, but the choice is restricted, not only to concentrate on the people whose work in their own gardens is especially admired, but also to see how gardeners with many decades' experience behind them have developed their planting styles and priorities over the years. The design and planting plan of Penelope Hobhouse's new garden reflect her search for simplicity combined with a richness and ebullience in the planting, learnt and developed from her many years at Tintinhull.

The foliage and form of plants has become at least as important to her as any flowers they may produce seasonally, a trait common to most of the other gardeners whose planting ideas are examined here. Rosemary Verey's concept of 'planting in layers' (see page 20) has been honed over the seasons in which she has observed her garden at Barnsley evolve. And in his bold experiments with colour, epitomized by the transformation of Great Dixter's old rose garden into a subtropical jungle, Christopher Lloyd has allowed his innate sense of adventure to lead the way.

The restrictions and accepted practices that have dominated gardening for decades have been rethought, dismissed or turned on their heads. As Beth Chatto has demonstrated in her own plantings, the bond between a garden and the natural landscape is inextricably linked and in a sense the garden has become a closer recreation of the natural landscape, an environment where the seasonal changes are relatively uninterrupted by human intervention, and plants that grow happily together in the wild are grouped together in a border or bed.

Growing indigenous plants, growing plants specifically because they naturally thrive in certain conditions, and developing plant colonies or landscapes rather than just a totally man-made setting of formal borders are all ideas that the book demonstrates to be of increasing importance today. And although the gardens featured are all in England, these ideas have far wider establishment: gardeners in the United States, Germany and Holland, in particular, are at the forefront of creating harmonious plant landscapes, and in many parts of the world this new approach to plants and planting is leading to a new appreciation of native flora.

The degree to which – more than at any time in the past – gardening cannot be labelled with certain styles and traditions is a central message of *Classic Planting*. New plant landscapes are growing up alongside borders of long-established formality; kitchen gardens, with their roots in the ways of the past, are undergoing a new emphasis on the integration of flower and vegetable planting; the opportunities offered by water and waterside planting have broadened to encompass the conscious formality of Tintinhull's long pool and the lush, predominantly foliage planting in and around Beth Chatto's naturalistic water garden.

In this light it is all the more revealing to study the work of gardeners who are all long-experienced and intimately familiar with the plants they grow. There is not one of them who would say that classic planting is easy to achieve. Forward planning, trial and error, and experiments are all inevitable. But each and every one stresses over and over again certain practicalities in which planting and plant associations must be firmly grounded. The need to be familiar with your soil – its composition and texture, its potential for improvement – and to choose the kind of plants it most readily supports, the fact that shade-lovers will not thrive in hot sun: these may sound self-evident and very basic, but such a commonsense approach is often overlooked. Beth Chatto aptly sums it up when she says: 'Disastrous results make you think you have a "problem" situation, when all you have is a site that different species of plant would enjoy.'

The priorities of adaptability and healthy, self-sufficient plants rather than demanding invalids result in a range of plants that appears over and over again in classic planting schemes. But, far from being boring or predictable, the repeated use of these 'high-performance' plants, suited to different conditions and to a wide variety of neighbours, leads to a liberating variety of approaches to planting. As Beth Chatto remarks: 'Two painters will take the same pigments and will produce an entirely different picture.' That many of these – in the best sense – popular plants contribute as much with their shape, texture and foliage as their flowers, and can be left with little interference from season to season, reveals much about the direction in which many contemporary gardeners are heading.

Each of the gardeners in *Classic Planting* would heartily agree that gardening is a never-ending process of instruction and education, of seeking new inspiration and being guided by example. Looking at their ideas, comparing and analysing their messages and advice, and applying the same principles of planting in your own garden should prove stimulating and rewarding.

SPRING PLANTING

'I THINK OF SPRING PLANTING AS A CONSTANT PAGEANT FROM WINTER TO SUMMER. SO MANY SPRING COMBINATIONS, FROM THE EARLIEST SUCH AS THESE CYCLAMEN, ACONITES AND SNOWDROPS, ARE UTTERLY NATURAL IN THEIR EFFECT AND THUS NEVER LOOK CONTRIVED. THEY SHOULD HAVE A PLACE IN EVERY GARDEN, LARGE OR SMALL.'

ROSEMARY VEREY

From winter into spring: aconites, snowdrops and *Cyclamen coum* with marbled green leaves carpet the ground beneath an old lime tree in Rosemary Verey's garden at Barnsley House.

For Rosemary Verey, the key to classic spring planting is combining a sense of natural succession and progress as the garden's season unfolds, making use of the individual qualities of different plants. Spring is the season that moves from the bleakness of winter to the luxuriance of summer and such change in the garden setting and framework can be reflected in planting. In the various borders and beds in her garden at Barnsley House the spring planting beneath trees and shrubs expands further each year as bulbs naturalize. The small early spring trio of cyclamens, winter aconites (*Eranthis hyemalis*) and snowdrops (*Galanthus nivalis*) beneath her lime tree all thrive under the protective, shady canopy that keeps off excessive rain in summer when they are setting seed (thereby spreading) and in a situation which guarantees minimal disturbance of the soil. No plant with either more extensive flowers or foliage would survive in this position, where the great network of tree roots commandeers virtually all available moisture; through the rest of the year the ground is shaded by the tree's umbrella of leaves and needs no decoration.

Planning a spring planting is perhaps the most enviable of the year. The season's unfailing freshness, enhanced by gradually strengthening light, gives individual plants the background against which to shine. Against a sparse and subdued background bare branches and earth are steadily transformed as a tapestry of new annual growth is unfolded. Spring colours are often muted, but the pale greens, creams and yellows are able to hold their own because they are not competing with vigorous foliage. At the same time, this is a season of surprising contrasts, and combinations can be bold: a mixture of apparent clashes such as red and orange wallflowers, purple and yellow tulips.

Our leading gardeners integrate spring planting into their border schemes, to provide a prelude to the summer planting that grows up to replace them, but the most natural spring planting is drifts of bulbs either steadily naturalizing in grass from year to year, or in a woodland type of setting, where bulbs and perennials thrive in the semi-shade around flowering shrubs or beneath trees that have not yet taken on their leafy canopies. An atmosphere

LEFT Garden or countryside? Daffodils (these are *Narcissus* 'February Gold') naturalize beneath silver birches in early spring before any sign of leaf and when the ghostly pallor of the birch trunks offers the greatest contrast with the yellow narcissi.

ABOVE Spring is often a season for bright colour combinations, as exemplified here with flame-flowered tulips beneath the branches of a purple-leaved berberis.

that is natural and uncontrived is an increasing priority for contemporary gardeners and at no time of the year is it more achievable than through the months of spring. Drifts of narcissi beneath white-stemmed birches may provide an ideal colour combination but, more importantly in today's garden, it is a scene that could just as well be in the countryside as in a garden.

Spring is a season of flowering extremes, when the blooms of magnificent flowering trees such as *Magnolia campbellii* are set against tiny, delicate-flowered bulbs clustering on the ground below. These two extremes are an important and recurring feature, providing the planting foundation for the spring garden which, once established, enable it to be the season when the gardener's hand should be the least noticeable. They express a precious quality of spring planting – the essentially natural character given by planting that evolves from year to year, rather than being annually replenished or reorganized.

It is this diversity of scale between trees and bulbs, rather than a wide variety of different plants, that offers an opportunity in spring planting scarcely possible in the rest of the year. The best range of ornamental woody plants – flowering trees such as magnolias and fruit trees; shrubs such as viburnums and daphnes – flower in spring or as the season merges into early summer. The potential for harmonious combinations using these structural plants with small bulbs and perennials is one that we will see being regularly repeated in different gardens.

Like Rosemary Verey, Penelope Hobhouse also planted drifts of small, early-flowering bulbs, but in her borders at Tintinhull they thrive in the half-shaded leafy soil around spring-flowering shrubs. 'Deciduous shrubs such as berberis, corylopsis, deutzias, dogwoods, hazels, philadelphus and viburnums work well in a mixed border,' she explains, 'sheltering low-growing spring bulbs with their canopies and allowing space for good clumps of perennials.' All the shrubs she describes have an attractive outline of bare wood before their foliage appears. Once in leaf they will prevent anything from growing beneath them and when they have flowered they provide form to offset the colour and leaf of the later perennials integrated into the planting.

When gardening at Tintinhull, Penelope Hobhouse especially liked to see broad carpets of blue scillas, chionodoxas and *Anemone blanda*, all of which thrive in well-drained ground beneath deciduous shrubs and, if left relatively undisturbed, will spread happily. Such combinations have a pleasing element of scale – the large, permanent framework of shrub or tree balancing the smaller, more fleeting bulbs – that characterizes much spring

planting. A spring-flowering viburnum such as *V. carlesii* or its delicate hybrid, *V.* × *carlcephalum*, both deliciously scented, combine perfectly both scale and the colour of their tight pink-flushed white flowers with the different bright blues of the bulbs.

The garden at Tintinhull also showed Penelope Hobhouse the adaptability of many small spring-flowering plants, such as the common wood anemone which grows wild to form dense carpets throughout deciduous woodland. 'Under the wall native wood anemones (*Anemone nemorosa*) are massed to produce a spring carpet of white and green, while the ground-hugging yellow-flowered *A. ranunculoides* yearly increases its spread and escaped seedlings – distributed by birds – of blue-flowered *A. apennina* appear everywhere. *Cyclamen repandum* seeds freely here

RIGHT Bold but harmonious intermingled groups of small flowers are essential to early spring planting. These yellow species crocus and purple *Cyclamen coum* display themselves above a carpet of marbled cyclamen leaves that sets off their bright colours.

LEFT Small-flowered narcissi are one of the most effective spring flowers for naturalizing in grass and beneath trees.

among clumps of Solomon's seal and crowns of creeping scented woodruff. This "natural" planting is given more formality with blocks of erythroniums, their shining leaves making focal points even before the flowers open their nodding heads in late spring.'

Perhaps without the groups of erythroniums, the planting that she describes could be as easily discovered in the wild as in the corner of a garden. The individual colours are often vivid, yet the white and blue anemones, bright pink cyclamens and creamy yellow erythroniums blend easily together and with their background of different foliage greens.

The idea of small flowering plants beneath shrubs and trees, creating the atmosphere of woodland early in the season before it is darkened by a full cover of leaves, is infinitely adaptable, whether at Tintinhull and Barnsley in the west of England or in Beth Chatto's garden across the other side of the country. Here,

the spring planting predominates in the shady areas: 'Most of the plants that grow well under my trees and shrubs are spring-flowering – they use the light before the leaf canopy comes. Shade gardens generally flower between March and June. The rest of the year the area will be predominantly foliage.' Before the foliage takes over, however, she has highlighted different areas of the shade gardens with mixtures, for instance of snowdrops, or leafy pulmonarias and epimediums. It is instructive to see her own description of one area of her shade garden, beneath the canopies of an oak and a holly:

'The first flowers often appear in January when the buds of *Narcissus minor* 'Cedric Morris' (brought home from Spain by the late Sir Cedric over thirty years ago) begin to open ... Other plants that flower in early March are the erythroniums. The dog's tooth violet (*Erythronium dens-canis*) is not the least like a violet.

Before the leaves
unfurl fully on
the trees, an
underplanting can
thrive in the light
that will not
penetrate the
canopy of foliage
later in the year.

These two planting details illustrate tulips in contrasting guises. To the left yellow tulips mingle informally with creamy cowslips among the meadow grasses, while below the picture is a more painterly composition of the lily-flowered tulip 'West Point' and forget-me-nots.

Its mauve lily-like flowers look much more like cyclamens when their pointed petals reflex in the warmth of early sunshine. They are followed by *Erythronium* 'Pagoda' and *E.* 'White Beauty', two hybrids of American erythroniums which are taller than *E. dens-canis* and have yellow and cream flowers. I plant drifts of them under the trees and shrubs. Visitors sometimes mistake them for small lilies … The last of my snowdrops are out at the end of March.'

Many of these plants can prove to be surprisingly adaptable and with Beth Chatto thrive in many differing conditions, including an area with three open sunny borders: 'All three beds contain plants which enjoy retentive soil and the open sunny site,' she explains. 'In spring there are bulbs, including our own native fritillary (*Fritillaria meleagris*) … also several species of narcissi and snowdrops as well as erythroniums, like *Erythronium dens-canis*, *E.* 'White Beauty', *E.* 'Pagoda' and *E. californicum*. All these plants like deep rich soil that does not dry out, although they would not tolerate the boggy conditions lower down the slope nearer the water's edge.'

Another feature of Beth Chatto's planting in shady areas is the use of spring-flowering ground-cover perennials. One she favours is the dwarf periwinkle (avoiding the larger *Vinca major* as too invasive.) '*Vinca minor* 'Variegata' makes attractive carpets of green and cream leaves, while others have blue, purple or white flowers, and there are double-flowered forms in blue and purple … I have *Vinca minor* 'Bowles Blue' around the base of *Hamamelis mollis*, making total cover beneath this wide-spreading shrub where it would be both laborious and boring to creep on hands and knees picking out regular crops of weeds.'

Through the spring, different areas of Beth Chatto's garden are carpeted with such ground cover: yellow-flowered ranunculus;

A classic combination of 'China Pink' tulips growing up through a blue mass of forget-me-nots, the colours given an unusual added dimension by the strong backdrop of the rheum foliage behind.

blue-flowered *Brunnera macrophylla* (whose heart-shaped leaves should be removed in summer when they become brown and leathery, allowing the new growth to take over) and epimediums with their overlapping layers of coppery green marbled leaves. These were once described to me as looking like the overlapping shields of a Lilliputian army, but they remind Beth Chatto of 'German roof tiles I have seen that look like fish scales'. Elsewhere is *Symphytum ibericum* (syn. *grandiflorum*), which Margery Fish described as 'the best of all the symphytums for ground cover' in her now classic *Ground Cover Plants*, but with the caution that 'some of the symphytums are frankly too coarse and invasive for any but the very wild places in the garden'.

As this small selection demonstrates so well, it is often the choice of plant and position which ensures enduring success. Margery Fish's warning about symphytums is well-founded and not only are they unsuitable for any position where their growth needs to be controlled, but the choice of variety is important. The same is true of periwinkles (*Vinca* spp.), but epimediums and brunneras, by contrast, are equally suitable as low edging along the front of a border as they are in a natural setting and the choice of variety can happily be left to personal preference.

Traditional gardening dogma made the distinction between a

concept of woodland or natural gardening, and border or arranged planting. The flowering trees, shrubs and bulbs of woodland gardening provided the springtime display, enjoying their peak before the foliage canopy closed in, by which time the summer borders would be conveniently coming into their own. Today we are being led by gardeners such as Christopher Lloyd and Beth Chatto to progress from this accepted idea of a clear difference between the concept of 'wild/woodland' and 'bed/border', or with classifying styles as formal or informal, and segregating plants associated with the two styles. Christopher Lloyd emphasizes that 'you should not pigeonhole plants' and at no time of the year is this more relevant than in spring.

In her garden at Barnsley, Rosemary Verey practises this merging of barriers and maintains a continuity throughout spring by what she calls 'planting in overlapping layers'. These layers are not only practical ones of adjacent plants at different heights or bulbs planted above one another, but also layers of time, giving a sense of constant unfolding through the season. For many gardeners, still confined by the weather to looking on their gardens from inside their homes, the intermingled carpet of bright-coloured aconites and snowdrops is a scene that belongs to winter, but flowering in such quantity is a sure sign that the garden is moving away from the isolated planting effects of winter and that the unfolding of layers has begun.

In Rosemary Verey's constantly moving spring pageant the unchanging structure and occasional highlights of the winter garden are replaced by an increasingly overlapping tapestry of plant combinations. Many are simple, but the variety of both form and colour is well illustrated by some of her favourite spring combinations: '*Tulipa* 'China Pink' offset by the spreading leaves of *Rheum palmatum rubrum*; the intensity of orange *Tulipa* 'Prinses Irene' with cowslips; daffodils beneath cherry blossom.' In the first there is exciting boldness in the contrast of the rheum's luxuriant foliage and the deliberate juxtaposition of its mauvy green undersides with the pink tulips (the deeper pink 'Mariette' as well as 'China Pink') growing out of a sea of forget-me-nots (*Myosotis*).

The companionship of strong orange and cowslip yellow is not an obvious one and yet at this time of year it is often successful – the orange and yellow of crown imperials (*Fritillaria imperialis*) would be another seasonal example of this sunny combination. White cherry blossom and narcissi combine in a classic spring scene, with, once again, the emphasis on extremes of scale so characteristic of the season.

Spring plant combinations extend throughout the garden at Barnsley and most appear in borders where they will be followed by a succession of later flowers – a reinforcement of the idea of planting in layers. Talking about one area close to the house, Rosemary Verey explains: 'Here, after Christmas, the bulbs begin to come through, accompanied by cowslips, forget-me-nots and hellebores … We keep to white, yellow and blue. The daffodils remain in and are allowed to increase from year to year. Each autumn we plant tulips, such as the vivid canary yellow 'Makassar' which flowers in early May, with Viridiflora 'Spring Green' tulips in front of them.' The daffodils remain, but to encourage the cyclical movement through the layers the tulips, forget-me-nots and cowslips are all moved out after they have flowered.

Another important feature of Rosemary Verey's spring planting (which we have seen in Penelope Hobhouse's and Beth Chatto's gardens) is how the same favourite plants are used over and over to create different effects. Another border close to the house, says Rosemary Verey, 'always has a generous carpet of white Dutch crocus which come up in February through the tulip and narcissus shoots. The tulips we keep to pink lily-flowered 'Mariette' and 'China Pink'. These look well with a dwarf *Prunus* that suckers through the border and blends with the young leaves of the *Berberis* × *ottawensis purpurea* which marks the south corner.' The same pink tulips that provided such an effective contrast with the unfurling foliage of the rhubarb-like rheum are now partnered with the more delicate effect of shrubs clothed in a haze of blossom pink and dark purple. In both of these plantings Rosemary Verey takes advantage of an often overlooked point: that some of the most successful spring plant combinations are

LEFT A simple group of 'Spring Green' tulips has a freshness that should always be a feature of planting for this time of the year.

RIGHT Low spring sunlight at Great Dixter adds brilliance to the different shades of 'West Point', 'Ballerina' and 'Dyanito' tulips and to the pure white of the late spring-flowering shrub, *Exochorda* × *macrantha* 'The Bride' behind.

those that include the fresh emerging foliage of other plants whose main season comes later.

These combinations and groupings are notable for their strong colours but elsewhere at Barnsley Rosemary Verey illustrates the subtleties of shape and colour that can be achieved with repeat groups of the same plants. Tucked against one wall of the garden is the winter walk, where a succession of different plant shapes is accentuated by the repeat shades of green and white, the overall effect outstandingly simple. Clipped box balls along the path give a permanent structure and, between them, carpets of aconites are

followed by a green and white tapestry of snowflakes (*Leucojum aestivum*) and green-flowered *Helleborus argutifolius*.

From the natural style, where the gardener's hand gently encourages the annual spread of spring bulbs that is so strongly evident in gardens such as Beth Chatto's, it is an intriguing contrast to move to Great Dixter. Here Christopher Lloyd integrates spring bulbs and perennials into his scheme for the long mixed border that extends away from one side of the house. But the garden is especially notable for the almost flam-boyant mass plantings, using wallflowers (*Erysimum cheiri*) and

tulips in bold single colour blocks. For most gardeners wall-flowers are unfailingly old-fashioned, best summed up by a description like Beth Chatto's of the perennial, and perennially popular, wallflower, *Erysimum* 'Bowles' Mauve': 'When I stoop to put my face into the velvet-textured, crumpled petals of old-fashioned wallflowers and smell the rich heavy scent I feel almost unbearably sad – the kind of feeling evoked only by reminders of childhood.' Close up, the wallflowers at Great Dixter retain such evocative qualities, but from a distance, arranged as they are in great blocks of colour, either close to or

in front of tulips in corresponding colours, they take on an altogether more imposing presence.

In some areas the wallflowers are planted with companion blocks of tulips, for instance the mauve shades of *Erysimum* 'Bowles' Mauve' complementing the similar but stronger-shaded tulip 'Greuze'. Throughout the garden these blocks of single varieties of tulips are arranged by colour in a brave but effective combination of adventure and subtlety. Against the framework of shrubs and the dark green of clipped yew in the long border they give a sense of perspective and progression more usually

LEFT One of the seasonal wonders of Great Dixter is wallflowers massed in monchrome blocks in the style of formally bedded summer annuals. Often, as here, they are matched by equally strong-coloured tulips.

RIGHT A random meadow effect in one of the beds of the parterre garden at Barnsley House, referred to by Rosemary Verey as 'my medieval flowery mead'. The soft pink tulip 'Apricot Beauty' flowers with bunched triple-flowered narcissi. The 'planting in layers' that is a priority in the garden comes with early crocuses before this combination and summer-flowering perennials later.

associated with the mixed flowering of later summer and autumn – there are shades of orange and bronze imparting a warmth that comes as a wonderful surprise at this time of the year. The same effect is produced by the rich red of 'Halcro' tulips on either side of a paved path in the old kitchen garden. Again, the background of clipped yew that is ever present at Great Dixter is the ideal foil to the tulips, the two deep and complementary shades interacting to perfection.

Like Rosemary Verey, Christopher Lloyd uses foliage to enhance the tulips' colours, but the effect could not be more different. At Barnsley the balance is between individual adjacent plants; here the impact is made by planting *en masse*, the blocks of single colours brought together by the dark green backdrop. Wallflowers used in such a way shed their cottage garden image and tulips gain an intensity so that the effect is comparable to massed summer annuals. And in a situation where they are to be followed by later flowering plants, they must be treated as annuals and removed after flowering. But for Christopher Lloyd the unseen work that goes on in late autumn and through the winter is always worthwhile once his tulips and wallflowers appear.

Tulips are a seasonal classic that, as we have seen, are an almost

indispensable part of the spring scene and yet widely adaptable. The garden designer Russell Page admitted to being a tulip addict and wrote that, 'devising colour schemes with tulips is a deeply satisfying task. I find myself again and again setting white and black-purple tulips on a ground of white violas or white daisies or occasionally the darkest blue forget-me-nots ... I like white, pink and red-feathered white tulips on a ground of dwarf double daisies, either red or white. You can add a quite strong scarlet tulip to this combination. Pink and scarlet tulips usually combine well, as do pink and scarlet dahlias later in the season.'

Most revealing about Russell Page's comments is the way in which he constantly returns to tried and tested favourite schemes with tulips, and Rosmary Verey agrees when looking at the planting in her garden: pink tulips against grey and silver foliage, or pinks, reds and white among the complementary colours of narcissi or blue-flowered bulbs. Among meadow grass the strength of colour of their individual flowers guarantees that they illuminate the whole scene.

The tulip's principal rival as the archetypal spring flower must be the narcissus. Not only do daffodil yellows represent the colour of the season, but narcissi have the potential to cross the barrier between the previously accepted styles of border and woodland planting that have been so inculcated in gardeners in the past.

For the most successful effects, however, choice of narcissus is important. Seasonal continuity will suffer, for instance, if you choose to plant heavy-headed hybrids for naturalizing. They

For many gardeners the foliage and flowers of different hellebores, such as the purple-flowered *Helleborus orientalis* shown here, are indispensable to spring planting – even becoming, as for Penelope Hobhouse, 'a grand passion'.

develop into thick blocks and throw up a mass of clumpy foliage that cannot be mown until early June. And Christopher Loyd warns that if you plant them in a border they will, 'in May, make your border look as though it is finished for the year, when it has not even begun.'

Such display daffodils are for planting in containers or where they will play no part in the garden's annual progress. Instead, for both naturalizing and being part of a more formalized border planting, species narcissi and the lower-growing, small-flowered varieties are invariably most effective. Describing one corner of her dry garden (where not many daffodils can thrive), Beth Chatto makes the point about her choice of *Narcissus triandrus* and *N. asturiensis*: 'Being small and with delicate flowers, they fit

far better with the low mats of thyme or artemisia than the big blowsy blooms of some of the cultivated and 'improved' narcissi.' At Tintinhull, the small-flowered narcissi that are naturalized in one area (and which characteristically spread in attractive drifts rather than in ungainly clumps) flower early in the year with aconites and crocuses, and therefore the grass can happily receive its first spring cut without fear of preventing the daffodils from setting their seed. Similarly, in a border group the small-flowered varieties (and species, such as *N. triandrus* or *N. cyclamineus*), flower in succession throughout the spring months when they will complement the small blue-flowered bulbs of the same weeks, and their foliage is sufficiently neat and restrained that while dying off it will quickly be concealed by emerging summer perennials.

One group of spring-flowering plants that have universal admiration from all who grow them is the hellebores, which Penelope Hobhouse has said 'could become a grand passion'. They are adaptable (although not to being moved) to the all-important theme, looking as at home in a woodland position as among spring-flowering plants in a border. Their bold (often evergreen) foliage provides a foil to brighter colours around them, and for many months of the year the different leaves are outstanding in their own right, especially, perhaps, the tooth-edged lime greens of the sculptural Corsican hellebore, *Helleborus argutifolius*, and the divided fans of darker green-leaved *H. foetidus*. Beth Chatto plants both these tall-growing hellebores for the manner in which their strong form and striking colours can make an impact from a distance. Only in late winter is the old foliage best removed, especially from the many different hybrids of *H. orientalis*, so as to show off the flowers whose saucer shapes are as subtly varied as their colouring, from creamy green to white and many shades of mauve almost to black. It is an indication of their quality that, despite their muted shades, Beth Chatto describes the orientalis hybrids as 'the most sumptuous of late winter and early spring flowers'.

The crowning attraction of hellebores is that, as well as their individual qualities, they are unfailingly good companions; it is almost impossible to think of a plant that is not shown to good effect as their neighbour. The same is true of euphorbias where, again, it is the varying shades of green rather than the seasonal flower colour that is primarily important. The spring garden can lack the solidity of plant shapes that is all too easily achieved later in the year, a shortcoming that the larger euphorbias such as the slightly tender honey spurge, *E. mellifera*, and the often indistinguishable hybrids of *E. characias* and *E. wulfenii* (now combined) will always overcome. As Penelope Hobhouse demonstrated with the repeat plantings of *E. characias wulfenii* in the borders of Tintinhull's Eagle Court, few plants give such sculptural form to a border in spring, especially when grouped with evergreen shrubs such as daphnes as the background to the brighter colours of transient flowers.

Such is the sense of progression through the weeks of spring that it is difficult to choose the time that is most representative, but the fritillary family exemplifies the interwoven strands of natural and formal, reticent and bold, that have become, in plant terms, the season's enduring qualities. First, the pungent smell of *Fritillaria imperialis*, the crown imperial, announces the arrival of spring, but more beguiling is the mysterious beauty of the native snakeshead fritillary, *Fritillaria meleagris* and other similar, but less widely grown varieties, their flowers of hanging bells in shades ranging from creamy green to deep chocolate purple.

Crown imperials are one of the most extraordinary spring flowers, their leaves almost too waxy and the deep orange and yellow bells below their topknots too rich for the time of year. But they rarely look out of place in a spring border, especially beneath the canopy of a white-flowering cherry to balance their thrusting, vertical lines, or in front of smaller, more modest, companions such as blue forget-me-nots, purple aubrieta or white arabis. Their strong shape means that they are also ideal for a more formal spring border – in groups they can bind together a pattern of smaller plants and emerging foliage in a comparable manner to, for instance, the blocks of tulips in Christopher Lloyd's long border at Great Dixter.

From the luxuriant qualities of the crown imperial to the fleeting, delicate and soft-shaded snakeshead is a transformation so marked that it is hard to believe they are related. Their growing habit is also quite different; *Fritillaria meleagris* being a native of water weadows favours a slightly shady, damp grassy position.

The gardening writer Robin Lane Fox nurtures fritillaries in his own Oxfordshire garden. A fellow of New College, Oxford, it was the sight of fritillaries in one of their most spectacular sites in the wild, the watery Christchurch Meadows beside the River

LEFT The harmonious emergence of yellow and mauve in the laburnum walk at Barnsley heralds the shift from spring towards summer. Beneath the intermingling racemes of laburnum and wisteria, the onion heads of *Allium hollandicum* reach up.

RIGHT Taking advantage of emerging summer foliage, these 'Palestrina' tulips are offset to perfection by the furry new growth of *Stachys byzantina* (syn. *lanata*) and silvery *Artemisia ludoviciana latiloba*.

Cherwell at Oxford, that prompted him to describe these favourite spring flowers as plants that he himself 'might rescue from the riverbed'. In the right conditions and when left undisturbed, they will naturalize rapidly, spreading their dappled shades of mushroom mauve and crinkled white. Native in the wild for centuries, they never lose their air of naturalness in the garden, these seemingly fragile yet strange intense little flowers encapsulate all the qualities of spring planting.

Such classic spring plants as tulips, narcissi, hellebores, euphorbias and fritillaries all have their own particular highlights. But they all appear, bloom and die away against a background of unfolding growth and change. For Penelope Hobhouse the essence of this change (which never loses its annual fascination and sense of expectation) is the prospect of new green shoots thrusting out of the bare earth, almost to the extent that now she

is 'more excited about the emerging greens of foliage' than by spring flowers themselves. Christopher Lloyd once memorably described the new growths as 'the snouts go shooting'. In a woodland setting it is perhaps the new fronds of ferns pushing through fallen leaves or growing up to replace dying snowdrop leaves. In a border this sense of regeneration is even more marked and, whether as a foil to spring flowers or alone, the picture of emerging summer growth is the vital catalyst to spring's progress. There is a freshness to the texture and shades of green in young hostas, delphinium shoots or the dumpy cushions of geraniums that cannot fail to enhance whatever is flowering in the vicinity. They mark the season's progress more emphatically than anything else because, once a majority of these different shades of foliage are fully unfolded and the buds of deciduous trees have opened into dense leaf, only then is spring truly over and summer begun.

BORDERS FOR SUMMER

'THE GLAMOROUS FACE OF GARDENING, A

CHANCE TO COMPOSE WITH GREAT SUBTLETY

OR DARING WICKEDNESS – AS YOU WILL.'

PAM LEWIS

One of the double herbaceous borders
at Arley Hall typifies the concept of
classic summer planting. A border of
this size gives room for generous groups
of plants, with vertical statements such
as the delphiniums and mauve *Allium
giganteum* between more dome-shaped
plants such as *Anthemis tinctoria*.
Variations of scale, as between the aptly
named *Cephalaria gigantea* and the
smaller *Astrantia maxima* contribute to
the overall harmony of the planting.

For many people the essence of summer borders is an array of roses, especially perhaps the climbing and rambling varieties and old-fashioned shrubs, their pure soft colours enhanced by scent. The months spent looking at the skeletal branches are all forgotten when, in spring, new foliage and buds appear with the promise of a few weeks of glory. But, for contemporary gardeners, the message with roses is integration; no longer to be grown in splendid isolation in military beds, but incorporated into mixed planting where they are given skirts of perennial foliage, clambered into by small-flowered clematis ('roses and clematis were made for each other,' says Christopher Lloyd) and able to perform to maximum satisfaction as the focus of a planting scheme. Repeat plantings of the same variety, using the best such as pink-flowered 'Fantin-Latour', 'Constance Spry' or 'Ispahan', white-flowered 'Iceberg' or 'Boule de Neige' or the indispensable hybrid musks such as 'Penelope' or 'Felicia', are more satisfying than a 'collection' of different but usually disparate-looking varieties.

Christopher Lloyd rightly points out the compatability of roses and clematis, and they have huge potential as climbing and rambling plants in a summer planting scheme. In days gone by climbers were used when there was a wall or other permanent structure to support them, but an enjoyable feature of the contemporary garden is the adventurous range of ways in which they are accommodated into borders – Rosemary Verey trains summer-flowering clematis over little pyramids of pea-sticks which, when integrated among border plants, make an effective contrast with bulkier clumps of shrub and perennial foliage. Clematis are without doubt the most widely adaptable of climbers and offer the greatest continuity as well as variety through the year and in many cases their rate of growth means that they can be added at a late stage. Rambling rose varieties, such as white-flowered 'Seagull', 'The Garland' or 'Rambling Rector' immediately add an air of establishment behind a border, or a sense of relaxation if allowed to tumble over an arbour or frame surrounded by well-ordered and grouped perennials.

Among climbers, summer-flowering honeysuckles and jasmine add the note of heady scent which should always be lingering over a garden in summer. Especially on a brick or stone wall, climbers are always most effective when they mingle together: honeysuckle woven into ivy, a small-flowered clematis peeping through the mauve or white potato flowers of a solanum; a large blue clematis among yellow or pink roses; or when allowed to run through dense foliaged wall shrubs such as ceanothus or pyracantha. In a situation without the ready-made support of walls, or – as at Barnsley – where there is no formalized 'front' and 'back' to a border, climbers trained over a frame can bring instant and much needed height into a border's middle.

Their potential unruliness is part of the charm of these summer-flowering climbers but, at the same time, this is when there are more choices than any other on which to base plant associations, and how they are chosen and grouped together will decide the sense of continuity and harmony they project in their season. An

LEFT Roses and clematis provide endless possibilities for combinations of colour and form. Here the vigorous white-flowered Viticella clematis 'Huldine' is entwined with 'Elizabeth of Glamis', a rewarding rose that flowers all summer.

RIGHT Variations in pink in the colour-schemed round garden at Sticky Wicket: lupins, astilbes, centranthus and hardy geraniums cluster around old-fashioned shrub roses.

underlying continuity, whether in massed foliage of hostas or alchemillas as a border frontispiece, or repeated groups of tall, prominent plants such as lupins, delphiniums or foxgloves, is often necessary for a summer border to retain the balance between exuberance, which should be part of the mood, and chaos, which results from an embarrassment of riches. There is always another year to grow some of the plants there was no room for, and tried and trusted favourites as a mainstay are usually more rewarding – and invariably better neighbours – than novelties.

Overcoming the threat of chaos does not necessarily mean limitations or restrictions that will make a border look underdone or regimented. Indeed, the term 'border' is used in the loosest possible manner – it can be traditional and of sufficiently formal design and proportions to have an architectural quality of composition, as do the classic herbaceous borders at Arley Hall, or it can simply be a series of groups of plants growing together in a designated area, as you will find in Beth Chatto's garden. At Arley the key to the borders' success is the manner in which they complement the overall setting, both in style and scale, of the yew hedges, central lawn and vistas at this Victorian country house. From early summer, as the plants develop their green foliage and flowers begin to emerge, if not in ranks, in associated groups that grow together to present an impressively three-dimensional effect and bring the whole composition to a zenith.

In Beth Chatto's garden the design style is quite different and in most areas the planting is not arranged for such a seasonal peak. None the less, to look across the gravel garden or one of the deep beds in the water garden at this time of year gives a similar impression of plants grouped and associated to emerge together with their summer flower colour, foliage textures and overall shape.

Successful planting of summer borders has to do with first, choices, and second, thinking of plants in groups. The qualities of individual plants are all too obvious as you gaze admiringly in the nursery at a character you have read about, searched for and now found. But is it a character suitable for the environment to which you propose to transplant it? Will it get on with the neighbours you plan to put it with? Do you have any idea who those neighbours are going to be? If the answer to any of these questions is no you may run into trouble, as Beth Chatto warns: 'Inspired by beautiful pictures of blue this and yellow that, [people] then go to the garden centre and buy plants they cannot resist, thinking that all the plants require is to be put in the earth. It does not occur to them that the plant may not like the situation.'

Although relatively small-scale the main border of Pam Schwerdt and Sibylle Kreutzberger's garden has a superb sense of fullness through the choice and juxtapositioning of different plants. In the background the feathery arches of *Stipa barbata* and purple-pink *Geranium psilostemon* are prominent in front of a tall backing group of delphiniums. *Dianthus* 'Laced Monarch', penstemons, the deep purple rose 'Charles de Mills', silvery blue *Eryngium alpinum* and *Allium caeruleum* all give continuity to the colour scheme, with contrast coming from the sharp variegated foliage of *Iris pallida* 'Variegata'.

The twin questions of choice and plant association are particularly relevant in a restricted area. At Eastgrove Cottage it is revealing to see how Carol Skinner's planting manages to combine a sense of ebullient fullness with reassuring orderliness. This is partly achieved by the use of shrubs such as roses to provide a structural focus for groups of perennials and by choosing these perennials with compatible flower colour and individual form. In their Cotswold garden, Pam Schwerdt and Sibylle Kreutzberger have applied a similar restraint to produce borders that are small but superbly full in summer. From the house the main areas of planting are on either side of a central lawn, both sides restricted in size. But the combination of focal plants such as shrub roses and grasses with harmoniously associated perennials produces a picture that manages to be lush without looking overcrowded.

Adventurous use of shape and colour is always part of the summer planting at Great Dixter. A spray of perennial grass partially screens the combination of pale yellow evening primrose (*Oenothora biennis*) and red *Crocosmia* 'Lucifer' with a block of pale blue *Campanula lactiflora* in the background.

The key is to have at least an overall plan before you start. Beth Chatto suggests, 'I think it is a good idea when planning a new border to make a list of the plants you will use, even if you do not make an actual plan.' Think of the effect you are wishing to achieve, the colours you wish to predominate, the types of plant you want to grow and a selection of the individual plants themselves. When beginning to plant one area of the garden at Barnsley called the broad border, not least because of its generous proportions, Rosemary Verey found it helped to make three proposed colour scheme groups for the plants: green and red, green and blue, and gold. If your scheme involves shrubs, small ornamental trees, or hedges either behind as a backdrop or in front as an edging, Rosemary Verey advises getting these in first. Talking about the same border: 'To make the proportions more manageable, I decided to have a semicircle of evergreens, related to each colour scheme and forming a three-dimensional pattern, two-thirds of the way back in each section. Four bronze-tinged *Cryptomeria japonica* 'Elegans' formed the semicircle in the "red" border.'

You will be able to find out which perennial plants need time to get established, but as you build up the border do it in coherent groups. This may involve large gaps for the first year or two, these can happily be filled with annuals whose success may easily prompt you, like Christopher Lloyd, to incorporate them with gusto. He recalls an occasion when annuals came to the rescue at Great Dixter: 'My enormous specimen of *Solanum crispum* 'Glasnevin', with a host of mauve potato flowers in summer, died one year after flowering, without leaving the customary suicide note. I have since filled in with annuals and biennials and so enjoy the gap that I have no immediate intention of a permanent planting.' Not only is growing from seed immensely satisfying, while

Very few of us have the ability to envisage a whole border at once. But we are all able to piece together the jigsaw, to which creating a border is comparable, in a series of compatible groups rather than isolated, single characters. The pieces of a jigsaw are all intrinsically linked because, although most do not fit next to each other they do, in the end, go together to make a harmonious picture. So should a border. Of course, many of us cannot create a border in a single season, not least because it may easily be too expensive. So how to build up a coherent picture over a number of years?

Beth Chatto's concept of a border may be less formalized than many other gardeners', but this early summer mixture of aquilegia and *Milium effusum* 'Aureum' shows no less thought given to her plant combinations.

the permanent planting goes from one season to the next, it is invaluable to be able to make necessary or refreshing additions to the canvas on a short-term basis – gardening without this opportunity for ringing the changes soon becomes humdrum.

For Christopher Lloyd, good gardening 'is not so much a question of what to plant as what to leave out,' echoing Russell Page's 'the art of composing a garden is a question first of selection and then of emphasis'. But Page was well aware of the beguiling temptations that pop up, despite the best of intentions, as you go along. 'To consider a herbaceous border is to consider the plants that will go into it – and this may lead to the frequent and pleasurable pursuit of red herrings. I am constantly tempted to lose sight of my theme and scale in my delight at secondary details of planting. One name leads by association to another and, unless you take care, a garden in which you intend to plan for colour quickly ceases to be a unity and turns into a miscellaneous assortment of perhaps charming incidents.'

Another important goal in a summer border is continuity – 'Continuity is the watchword,' Christopher Lloyd counsels. This continuity is two-fold, first among the plants themselves and second from one week to the next as the border's growth evolves, the changing shapes and heights of foliage, emerging and disappearing shades of flower colour. In the early stages it is easy, no garden picture is more beguiling than the landscape of virginally fresh greens along a border: new leaves on structural shrubs beneath which spring bulbs are dying off, the edible-looking lime green shoots of delphiniums, low domes of different textured hardy geraniums that will either keep a dense habit or spread out in a more lax manner, unrolling hostas and ferns. But when the peonies – such a rich, blowsy feature of early summer – have

finished flowering and their leaves are getting brown along the edges, when the old-fashioned roses finish flowering abruptly, this is the test of the success of inbuilt continuity, to progress gracefully to the next stage.

In planning for continuity considerations of flower colour are secondary. The major constants are the permanent greens (and silvers, greys or variegated shades) of foliage and the plant shapes and textures. Shades of green ranging from nearly blue and purple to yellow, arching sprays and clambering stalks, domes, tall spires, dense blocks, spreading carpets – all these will bulk out a border throughout summer while tints of pink or blue, white or yellow come and go. They are the background against which any colour scheme should be woven. A crucial element of the weave can be contributed by plants specifically chosen because they will self-seed, and their value is something constantly emphasized. In today's gardens the element of informality that these opportunistic seedlings suggests, the idea of natural, uncontrolled regeneration, strikes a note of pleasing harmony. 'Once the planting is established,' comments Beth Chatto, 'I like to see plants run into one another a little or seed themselves. I do not always plant in defined groups of three of five, but may drop one or two of the plants further away as though they had seeded themselves. Even if I do not do that, nature will often take a hand and do it for me, and it seems sensible to let it happen, because it looks much more natural and attractive.' Penelope Hobhouse agrees. 'I find that a practical approach to managing mixed borders, in which every iota of soil should be covered with plants, is to encourage proliferation of self-sown seedlings. They will extend the theme adopted for any one area, fill every empty space and, allowed to flower, give the attractive and seemingly unplanned natural look that I am always seeking.'

Penelope Hobhouse finds that an important means of gaining continuity is by 'lots of repetition rather than too many self-conscious colour schemes'. In the light of this it makes a fascinating study to look at the two main borders in the pool garden at Tintinhull. Facing each other across the long central pool, they have been redeveloped since the 1980s from Phyllis Reiss's original planting during the late 1940s. Almost everywhere else in the garden at Tintinhull the borders are planned to begin with spring bulbs and continue without break into summer. Here in the pool garden, however, these are solely summer borders where, explains Penelope Hobhouse, 'more recently we have abandoned any early bulbs but allow the mixed greens and textures of emerging perennials, framed by a few early-flowering shrubs, to give us quieter pleasure.'

The borders do have overall colour scheming, on the one side 'hot' and on the other side 'pale'. But given the large scale and the fact that the desired effect runs right through, rather than in progressing patches, the scheming is unfussy and allows for strong interlocking plant statements. In the hot border the repetition that Penelope Hobhouse suggests is provided by groups of the red-flowered shrub rose 'Frensham': 'The 'Frensham' roses remain a mainstay of the whole border, particularly spectacular in June, but blooming in bursts throughout the rest of the summer.' Along with the roses the original replanting included green-leaved cotinus, variegated snowberries (*Symphoricarpos albus*), *Potentilla* 'Gibson's Scarlet' and tall orange lilies. But, as Penelope Hobhouse reflects, border-making for summer is a constant evolution and there has to be room for changes from year to year. 'Like all detailed plans which include a mixture of shrubs and perennials, these blueprints were only a start. Each season then, usually in spring, we move groups about to get relationships right and try new combinations.'

Given the shades of colour involved, many of these combinations are adventurous – the purple-leaved loosestrife, *Lysimachia ciliata* 'Firecracker' (syn. 'Purpurea'), in front of the 'Frensham' roses, for instance, is sensational in its contrast of shapes and the rich blending of leaf and flower colours. Other strong reds and purples – the late summer *Crocosmia* 'Lucifer', various red-flowered tender shrubby salvias, and *Lobelia* 'Dark Crusader', with spires of red flowers above dark purple foliage – are balanced by cooler shades and shapes. Great sprays of *Crambe cordifolia* on either side of the central recess decorated by an armillary sphere are like a refreshing shower, and the creams and yellows of camassias, a herbaceous, non-climbing clematis, *Clematis recta*, and × *Solidaster luteus* offset the fiery oranges from rudbeckias and others that become more evident later in the summer. Continuity between plants is balanced by continuity through the season: 'There are few late-flowering red shrubs and perennials to take over when 'Frensham' leaves off, so annuals and tender shrubby plants such as the salvias are important to keep the scheme going. We often use dahlias such

Summer flowers and foliage give a sense of luxuriance that flowers alone would never bring. Here, the effect is achieved with great stretches of foliage, including ligularias, grasses and ferns, against which are set the pale spikes of *Persicaria bistorta* and the bright oranges and yellows of hemerocallis and candelabra primulas.

as 'Bishop of Llandaff' and 'Bloodstone' which fill in during the latter half of the season.' Among the various plants, the vital ingredient of natural integration is supplied by self-seeding plants such as mulleins (*Verbascum* spp.) which, with the red-tipped pokers of kniphofias, accentuate the vertical accents along the border.

The contrast between the hot border and the pale one opposite is fundamental, and yet subtle continuity is provided by a selection of plants suitable to both, in particular silver foliage and shades of cream such as philadelphus (which would be suitable for any summer border scheme) and the small annual tobacco plant, *Nicotiana langsdorffii*, which fills in gaps with its delicate creamy green flowers. Penelope Hobhouse makes the point that while hot reds and oranges and bright yellows are colours from one sec-

tion of the palette and the choice of plants is therefore immediately limited, with pale shades the candidates multiply: 'Indeed, there are so many perennials to choose from that selection and repetition is the key; without this the whole scheme would collapse into bland chaos.' Repetitions of single plants making large groups bind the border together: blue-flowered *Galega orientalis*, white spires of the prolific willowherb, *Epilobium angustifolium album*, soft blue asters recurring near the front of the border with pink diascias, and bushes of the pure white-flowered *Rosa rugosa* 'Blanc Double de Coubert' symmetrically placed on either side of the bench that divides the border in half.

The pale flower colours of many perennials is balanced by their habit, either forming expansive clumps such as pink-flowered

LEFT Overall symmetry and strong combinations are the hallmarks of planting in the hot border at Tintinhull, with 'Frensham' roses used effectively in repeat plantings.

ABOVE The symmetry is complemented in the cool border that faces it across the pool, while the dramatic variation in planting typifies the diversity of Tintinhull.

goat's rue (*Galega officinalis*), or with bold flower shapes and striking foliage such as the creamy spires of *Cimicifuga racemosa* above its rosetted leaves. Feathery domes of artemisias are balanced by stronger shapes such as the silvery thistle-like *Eryngium giganteum*. Among the perennials and annuals the shapes of shrubs – deutzias, philadelphus and *Viburnum plicatum* 'Mariesii' – act as anchors for the composition. As in the hot border opposite, self-seeding pink and mauve poppies and the unusual cream-flowered *Collomia grandiflora* add the vital note of natural, un-artificed progression.

The hot and pale borders at Tintinhull are classically proportioned long rectangles, each backed by a yew hedge and fronted with stone edging and then lawn. Their originality lies in the plant combinations, well-known favourites mixing with rarities but all suited to the conditions. Their juxtaposition on opposite sides of the pool garden intensifies the contrast of their individual plantings. At Barnsley there is also a formal arrangement of borders close enough to interrelate and yet consciously planted for individuality. Whereas Tintinhull's pool garden borders are an enclosed entity, linked to other areas only by vistas through openings in the enclosing hedges, Rosemary Verey refers to her 'parterre' beds at Barnsley as 'the heart of the garden', surrounding as they do the main lawn in front of the house and bracketing its corners in four deep L shapes. (The description 'parterre' was given to them by the distinguished garden writer, Arthur Hellyer, and refers to their formal, symmetrical arrangement around the lawn, rather than the idea of the flat geometric planting traditionally associated with parterres.) Unlike the pool borders at Tintinhull, the summer colour in these parterres follows on – and flows on – from dense spring flowering.

While they are not consciously colour-schemed, each bed has its own character of planting as well as linking with the others, principally perhaps by the seemingly carefree intermingling that encourages easy continuity between the plants and through the months. The informality is encouraged by the borders' positions and shapes: they are viewed from both front and back and, with

LEFT Different leaf shapes and colours provide the setting for summer flowers at Barnsley. A hedge of golden privet, *Ligustrum ovalifolium* 'Aureum', forms the background, with delphinium spires breaking above its line. In the foreground yellow pansies mix with *Nigella damascena*.

RIGHT A wonderful juxtaposition of orderliness and summer ebullience where Barnsley's herb garden merges with the adjacent border in front of the garden's boundary wall.

the exception of one smaller than the others, their shape suggests a more amorphous planting style than a progression from one end of a vista to another.

The smallest bed lies in front of the house and joins at right angles with the herb garden that makes one side of the bed's L, leading to a side door. An important priority was to be able to see over the planting in both directions and so in summer it is predominantly a free-mixing composition of perennials, with annuals to fill in gaps left by spring bulbs. The colour shades are pink, blue and purple, white and yellow, all blending together and given continuity by repeats in different places of single plants such as the hardy little *Geranium sanguineum*, purple-tinted *Euphorbia*

amygdaloides robbiae, and annually planted *Penstemon* 'White Bedder' and white cosmos. Rosemary Verey confirms why hardy geraniums are such invaluable and accommodating border plants: 'The geraniums are those "easy plants" that Norah Lindsay recommended me to grow. Besides being easy, they are also such good value, flowering all through spring and summer; then in autumn their leaves turn a dazzling bronzy red.'

There are drifts of nigella or love-in-the-mist, whose pale blue flowers are followed by striking seedheads, aquilegias, astrantias and the tighter shapes of mauve-flowered tradescantias. As with the other beds, although in this one the overall scale of the individual plants is quite small, it is clear that they have been chosen with an eye for interesting form. The purple spires of *Salvia nemorosa* 'Ostfriesland', the elegant late-summer stems and blue flowers of agapanthus, and the domed silver of *Artemisia ludoviciana* are good examples of this use of shape, and it is especially evident on the prominent corners where there the spikes of *Sisyrinchium striatum* provide a full stop at one end, echoed by a grey dome of santolina at the other.

The planting in the bed facing has developed around the existing anchors of old evergreens, to which have been added other shrubs, including philadephus and *Buddleja davidii*. A key priority for this group of borders is to provide a sense of introduction to the rest of the garden, on to which they open in different directions, and so to one side, where a secluded little pool garden lies in front of a classical temple (see page 106), the planting was consciously built up to make a screen. Here there are some hotter colours, such as the black-eyed brilliance of the pink-purple *Geranium* 'Ann Folkard' but, as Rosemary Verey emphasizes, the background tapestry of foliage is the vital element, the greens having sufficient strength to bind together colours in strong and often dissimilar tones. It is interesting to see how the chain of ideas from one gardener to another continues: 'The idea of having orange alstroemerias with magenta *Geranium psilostemon*,' confesses Rosemary Verey, 'came from a recommendation in Graham Stuart Thomas's classic book, *Perennial Garden Plants*.'

There are also combinations of height rising from strong foliage such as groups of delphiniums with acanthus, and the unforgettable late-flowering *Salvia uliginosa*. As with the other beds, the medley gives a cottage-garden atmosphere, encouraged by leafy lamiums, pale hardy geraniums, the grey woolly leaves of *Stachys byzantina* (syn. *lanata*), drifts of honesty (*Lunaria annua*). Temporary height comes from bronze fennel (*Foeniculum vulgare* 'Purpureum'), *Crocosmia paniculata* and *Lobelia × gerardii* 'Vedrariensis'. The colours are also well composed, so that the occasional cool white of the luxuriantly tall *Campanula latiloba alba*, and the soft but intense yellow of one of the most striking plants, a tree lupin (*Lupinus arboreus*), increase the impact of brighter tones such as the orange oriental poppies (*Papaver orientale*) – not always easy to accommodate. Rosemary Verey comments: 'Oriental poppies are difficult to find the right companions for, but I must grow them for their wonderful buds, their crêpe paper-like petals and the way they

LEFT Although a bright pink, *Geranium* 'Ann Folkard' is an easier mixer than its more strident parent, *G. psilostemon*, and the slight golden overlay to the leaf colour always adds interest to a border.

ABOVE *Clematis* 'Lawsoniana', an old cultivar, displays a succession of elegant flowers that fade gracefully as they age.

Rather than using the pale yellow spires of tree lupin (*Lupinus arboreus*) to illuminate a cool blue or pastel colour scheme, Rosemary Verey has created a stunning eyecatcher by teaming them with flame-coloured poppies.

attract every bumblebee into the garden … The poppies and the tree lupin vibrate together with their bold colours.'

The two beds facing both have a backbone of flowering and evergreen shrubs to form a screen, but not a complete division, from the open lawn that lies on the far side, with the meadow grass and trees of the wilderness beyond. As well as the intrinsic value of shrubs such as the striking *Cotinus coggygria*, they contribute to a strong backdrop for the summer plants.

Rosemary Verey has described the bed furthest from the house as 'a controlled meadow garden' and it is revealing to see her description of some of the intermingled planting of shubs and perennials with annuals. 'Plants like the lovely evening primrose, *Oenothera biennis*, are allowed to put themselves where they wish, seeding one year and flowering the next. The beautiful but invasive *Campanula glomerata* competes with *Achillea ptarmica* 'The Pearl' and *Acanthus spinosus* – all strong growers that need controlling. For late interest the tall *Chrysanthemum uliginosum* [now *Leucanthemella serotina*] act as a background for a wonderful blue *Aster amellus* and *Cornus alba* 'Sibirica' … Hebes are among the most useful border shrubs, and here *Hebe rakaiensis* creates a rounded full stop on the narrow end. We drop in the intense blue *Salvia patens* as well as *Penstemon* 'Garnet' wherever there is a gap.'

In the bed facing, which on one side edges the house terrace, daisy-flowered argyranthemums, cosmos and tobacco plants (*Nicotiana*) are used to fill gaps. As well as the cotinus, the generous forms and shapes of other shrubs are especially prominent here, with some, such as the yellow pineapple-scented *Cytisus battandieri* and white philadelphus, adding to the summer flowering. As with the other beds, the choice of plants for form is clearly evident: spikes of echiums follow slender astrantias, and the later contribution of the graceful *Fuchsia magellanica* are good examples for different stages of summer. The informality of aquilegias and sweet rocket (*Hesperis matronalis*) threading through the border heightens the effect of some of the more unusual plants, such as the handsome *Aruncus dioicus*, whose clump of rosette leaves is topped by creamy white beards resembling a large astilbe.

Rosemary Verey's style of planting retains a jostling, cottagey flavour in her 'parterres', and the flexibility of summer planting is shown by the manner in which the round garden at Sticky Wicket has a similar character, despite being more obviously colour-planned. Pam Lewis has created the round garden principally with well-known but indispensable summer favourites such as aquilegias, irises, lupins, foxgloves, campanulas and phloxes, enlivened by rarities such as *Cimicifuga simplex* 'Brunette'. Part of the garden's interest derives from its unusual composition, which she describes as: 'paths radiating from a

camomile lawn, segmenting the floral ring of colour. Flowing from pastel pink, pale yellow and blue, round to violet then magenta and deepening to red shades with dusky pinks that bring the wheel full circle … The web of paths allows close contact with and observation of the plants.'

Colour control of this kind is notoriously hard to achieve and it is perhaps because Pam Lewis uses predominantly perennials whose shapes suggest a feeling of natural flow, that the movement from the colour shades of one area to another has an impression of being quite unregimented, the shift around the palette gently impressing itself rather than being strikingly evident. Planned to grow steadily to a peak in summer and to be sustained well into autumn by late-flowering perennials, the round garden's success also derives from Pam Lewis's choice of familiar plants rather than less accommodating rarities.

Sticky Wicket's round garden is a good example of how repetition can bring about the sense of continuity advocated by Penelope Hobhouse. Another important factor is the grouping together of more than one specimen of a plant, something urged by Beth Chatto: 'Quite often people fail to be bold enough in their plant groupings, and then do not get the full effect.' In some parts of the round garden selected plants are massed to spectacular effect, such as knautias in shades of purple and, in late summer, clumps of asters and verbena. But much of the subtlety of the shifting colour shades comes from choosing varieties from the same family: different buddlejas, campanulas, hardy geraniums, lavenders, salvias and achilleas all encourage the sense of continuity and a satisfying harmony.

Like Rosemary Verey, Pam Lewis has looked to flowering shrubs for added substance. Perhaps most prominent among these are the shrub roses, whose colour and shape act as focal points for plant associations. Many of the beds in the round garden have roses chosen to integrate with the different shades of colour that surround them. In one bed is deep purple 'William Lobb' and 'Roseraie de l'Haÿ' complementing *Buddleja davidii* 'Black Knight' with other similarly dark-shaded flowers such as purple *Verbena hastata* and *Salvia* × *sylvestris* 'Mainacht'. In another, where the colour theme is strong pink, an old pink moss rose blends with pink lavender, *Cistus* 'Silver Pink' and the striking *Centaurea montana* 'Carnea'. In a third the subtle plant associations have a hint of devilishness as the startlingly white flowers of the shrub rose 'Nevada' stand out among the blue and mauve haze created by lavenders, salvias and hummocks of hardy geraniums.

For the weeks of summer the gardener's palette is almost limitless, a treasury of possibilities including every imaginable type of plant: shrubs like philadelphus flowering deliciously, climbing roses and clematis, all manner of shrub roses, perennials, annuals and a selection of bulbs. At the same time there is a sense that the garden is galloping towards its mid-summer zenith, when, as the ground is properly and permanently warm, growth is inexorable. With this combination of profusion and natural energy control is essential, not now because it is too late, but in the original planning and the preparatory months, when the work you put in on your border will reap rewards when you want them.

LEFT When the planting at Sticky Wicket reaches its summer zenith, massed perennials provide a carefully planned progression of colours and shapes, as demonstrated by the allium seedheads in the foreground and banks of hardy geraniums beyond.

ABOVE The sculptural bluish leaves of *Euphorbia rigida* mixing with pinky-mauve *Geranium cinereum subcaulescens* and *Viola* 'Eastgrove Twinkle' show how foliage can add strength to a combination of flowers.

THE COLOURS
OF AUTUMN

'AUTUMN IS A TIME FOR BOLD COLOUR CONTRASTS.'

ROBIN LANE FOX

A group of perennials that all flower
well into autumn: *Salvia coccinea* 'Lady
in Red', *Verbena rigida*, *Aster sedifolius*,
Viola cornuta 'Alba', *Allium cristophii*
and *Libertia ixioides*.

Autumn, like spring, is a season of transition. We see the first signs as summer turns, often with the effect of weeks of heat and little moisture taking their toll on the garden, and the season continues through a period of diminishing light and temperature until the advent of regular frosts announce that winter has arrived. Autumn planting should reflect this sense of transition and does so most effectively when extended through the garden's whole spectrum.

One of the most significant developments in the contemporary garden is the extent to which autumn has grown to be enjoyed as a season in its own right rather than being seen principally as a period of decline from summer and a preparation for winter. Part of the impetus for this development comes from the growing appreciation of the natural cycle within a garden, so that perennials or foliage plants are chosen not only for their flowering quality but also because they continue with attractive foliage changes or seedheads through the season. This priority has, for instance, popularized the use of the perennial grasses Beth Chatto favours so highly, the myriad varieties giving superb shape and texture through the autumn garden.

At the heart of these developments is the belief that the human guidance of a garden through the seasons should combine harmoniously with – and at times defer to – the natural cycle, rather than being principally aimed at controlling it. In this light there is

LEFT The idea of a natural meadow landscape is perfectly extended into early autumn by this carpet of *Vicia cracca*.

ABOVE Hardy geraniums that have flowered in summer add to the autumn garden with marbled foliage tints. Their changing shades are balanced here by the permanence of evergreen *Skimmia japonica* behind, whose shiny leaves are further enlivened by warm red berries.

has influenced the growing appreciation of a number of plants, such as crocosmias and watsonias, that need the maximum possible period of summer sun and warmth to develop and then flower from late summer through autumn.

The visible impact of these changes in the perception of the autumn garden is most boldly revealed in the context of colour. The instinctive reaction of many gardeners is to relate autumn colour solely to the brilliant hues of foliage on ornamental trees and shrubs. The foliage of *Cercidiphyllum japonicum*, *Nyssa sylvatica* and all the captivating maple family and can indeed be splendid, but the wrong weather can entirely spoil the anticipated glory. Many are 'plant and wait' candidates, often not performing for years, while others are only really suitable for a large garden able to accommodate them in a setting of the right proportions.

Instead, the bold colours that Robin Lane Fox refers to on page 51 are those of border plants – annuals and perennials – and it is through combinations of these that the autumn garden is undergoing a deserved renaissance. It is a revealing thought that the main border in Gertrude Jekyll's garden at Munstead Wood was planted to begin flowering only in late summer and to continue through the autumn. She recognized a crucial element of the planting potential for this time of year when she wrote: 'Much of its beauty now depends on the many non-hardy plants, such as Gladiolus, Canna and Dahlia, on Tritomas of doubtful hardiness, and on half-hardy annuals.' She goes on: 'The Dahlia's first duty in life is to flaunt and to swagger and to carry gorgeous blooms well above its leaves …', suggesting the kind of characteristics that enable plants to dazzle away what all too many gardeners dismiss prematurely as a time to allow the garden to die back in anticipation of winter.

Dying back would certainly be far from your mind if, on a September day, you walked into the walled garden of Hadspen House, hidden away in a wooden coombe. Sandra and Nori Pope have gardened here for a decade, and in a garden brimming with good plant combinations perhaps the most admired feature is the border that stretches in front of the garden's unforgettable curving

enjoyment to be had from the period when plants that have peaked earlier in the year move towards winter. 'I enjoy the gradual change in hosta leaves from green, blue or variegated to warm shades of honey and amber,' says Beth Chatto, 'with, perhaps, a few overhanging leaves of Solomon's seal that turn bright yellow before they all collapse in sorry heaps.'

This emphasis of the garden's natural cycle has become an important influence on planting for autumn. It has encouraged an open-minded approach to the choice of plants that has both expanded the season's palette and revived plants that had become unfashionable, such as Michaelmas daisies. A key factor is working towards permanent or semi-permanent plant communities which

LEFT Hadspen's full glory: the curving border at the time when late summer merges into autumn. Nasturtiums (*Tropaeolum majus*) clamber up the wall and *Dahlia* 'Bishop of Llandaff' is prominent among the rich shades that are repeated the length of the magnificent planting.

RIGHT Flame-coloured nasturtiums spilling across the gravel path that fronts Hadspen's long walled border vie for attention with the fiery spikes of the suitably named *Crocosmia* 'Lucifer'. Further back, the velvet-rich petals of the climbing rose 'Altissimo' are echoed by the even darker foliage of *Prunus* × *cistena*.

walls, down from the entrance gate and back up from the bottom of the coombe. It is arranged in merging colours, from yellow to orange, red, plum, pink, peach and back to yellow.

In the areas of softer hues – pink and peach, for instance – much of the planting is for traditional summertime. The areas of hotter, brighter shades, however, seem to pick up in late summer and reach their peak in autumn. One vital factor is the combination of permanent plants such as crocosmias with those requiring annual attention such as dahlias. Both are evident among the oranges and reds, extending into the rich shades of plum: the crocosmias 'Star of the East', 'Flamenco', 'Lucifer' and 'Emily McKenzie'; the dahlias 'David Howard', 'Bishop of Llandaff', 'Arabian Night', 'Summer Night' and 'Black Diamond'. Equally strong colour is given by yellow and orange heleniums and helianthus, the red of *Fuchsia* 'Riccartonii' that adorns wild hedges in Ireland and the west coast of Scotland, or the plum-black of *Astrantia major* 'Hadspen Blood', raised in the garden's nursery. All along the border the richness of

colour is sometimes offset, sometimes enhanced, by the dense mass of intermingling foliage – much of it strong sword shapes of a boldness to match the colours: the crocosmias and sharp irises, euphorbias, phormiums and day lilies.

The Popes' success in creating a series of bold autumn effects in the planting at Hadspen is continued in the rodgersia border made against another wall of the main garden. Containing a comprehensive range of rodgersias that together constitute the National Collection, the border confirms the contemporary interest in seasonal peaks for this time of year. Rodgersias produce wispy, astilbe-like flowers in shades of cream and pink earlier in the summer, but their chief quality is their foliage, all large-scale and ranging from deeply cut or pinnate to leaves like scalloped dinner plates. They present a tapestry of different hues as they develop through autumn towards winter, with deep greens becoming tinted with chocolate brown or purple; in some, such as *Rodgersia podophylla*, the late autumn cold and damp bring out

LEFT Autumn colour exemplified – not the foliage of many gardeners' minds, but a powerful flowering combination of *Dahlia* 'David Howard' and mauve *Verbena bonariensis*.

RIGHT Brilliance and lushness through the autumn characterize the replacements for the ancient roses in the walled garden at Great Dixter. In the foreground is mauve-flowered *Verbena bonariensis* and the large purple-brown leaves of cannas. Behind are richly coloured dahlias – 'Alva's Doris' and 'Wittemans Superba' – and tall orange cannas.

brilliant shades of orange-red that survive to be enhanced by early frost. The overall effect is intensely textural and full of form to a degree that many gardeners would not imagine possible at this time of the year.

The adventurous nature of the Popes' planting at Hadspen is hinted at by Christopher Lloyd when he says 'people are frightened of orange'. He certainly is not – nor of the other hot colours that help the garden at Great Dixter flourish as strongly in autumn as in summer. Describing herbaceous phloxes he writes, 'It is easy enough to get your cool background shades and interesting shapes in the August border, but you really do need heavy splodges of colour to set these off. For this reason I don't mind phloxes of the most screaming pinks, mauves and magentas, as many of the old-fashioned sorts are.' A host of other autumn-flowering plants provide the punctuation marks of colour through Great Dixter: clumps of upright kniphofias and arching crocosmias given added impact by being planted on the edge of the raised terrace in the barn garden; orange, yellow and rich

cream ginger lilies (*Hedychium* spp.), blue and deep purple salvias against every shade of orange.

Shape, colour and texture are ever present in Great Dixter's planting at this time of year, confirming the thoughtfulness – and often the pioneering spirit – that goes into the plant combinations. There is a considered harmony of contrasts in a grouping around, for instance, the giant reed grass, *Arundo donax*, its bluish leaves arching behind spires of pink-red gladioli which reach up from an underplanting of the late-flowering forget-me-not, *Myosotis scorpioides*. Either side of a path in the old kitchen garden, hedges of the small-flowered and long-lasting *Aster lateriflorus* 'Horizontalis' have the low growing pink spikes of *Persicaria vacciniifolia* in front and contrast superbly with the purplish pink bells of angel's fishing rods (*Dierama pulcherrimum*) as they curve gracefully above.

But Great Dixter's autumn zenith is presented in the small enclosure that was once a demure rose garden. Some of the exotic foliage of, for instance, the castor oil plants (*Ricinus communis*) and

bananas, may have lost a little freshness since mid-summer, but the leaves have grown in size while the flowering plants are producing great splashes of colour. The red and orange cannas require weeks of hot sun to really perform and thus come into their own only as summer is coming to an end. Continuity through many weeks is provided by the purple of tall self-seeding *Verbena bonariensis*, and orange of corn marigolds (*Chrysanthemum segetum*) running as a brilliant, unusual bi-colour theme. The demise of Great Dixter's rose garden may have had some traditionalist admirers of the garden shuddering. But the replacement of a planting scheme that was tried, tested and, in many ways, tired, with such an adventurous arrangement only goes to emphasize the success that can be had in any garden by taking advantage of a sunny, sheltered enclosure to extend summer planting right through the autumn and to enjoy plants of doubtful hardiness in the way that Christopher Lloyd has done.

Fashion in flowers comes and goes. Bright orange flowers are often dismissed as vulgar in both form and colour but as Christopher Lloyd demonstrates, the right variety used in the right context and with plants that can match their vivid colour, can be well integrated and enormously effective. Rosemary Verey capitalizes on the brilliance of orange flowers by growing both marigolds (*Calendula officinalis*) and nasturtiums (*Tropaeolum majus*) among the lush greens of her kitchen garden.

Revisit the pool garden at Tintinhull late in the season and the hot border is alive with the strong yellows of achilleas and rudbeckias, red and orange crocosmias and orange and yellow kniphofias or red hot pokers, while dark red or purple dahlias that have been grown on in the kitchen garden are moved out into suitable positions to replace early summer features that have died back. Throughout the garden, Penelope Hobhouse developed the planting to extend seamlessly from summer through autumn. Because of the compartmented nature of the garden this can be achieved in a variety of ways in different areas, but there is a noticeable priority for using plants that perform at their best in these weeks. In the middle garden clumps of pink and white

Anemone × hybrida (syn. *japonica*) are offset by hydrangeas and the turning shades of arched fronds of Solomon's seal (*Polygonatum multiflorum*); on either side of the main kitchen garden path are the mixed mauves of *Malva moschata* and *Verbena bonariensis*, self-seeded between the domes of brilliant blue-flowered caryopteris, one of the best autumn-flowering shrubs. Across the pool from the hot reds and oranges, late-flowering perennials such as *Gaura lindheimeri* come into their own in the pale border, in combination with silvery blue, thistly heads of eryngiums, the soft silver of artemisias and the distinctive woolly seedheads of *Epilobium angustifolium album* that replace the plants' spires of white flowers. A theme here through late summer and autumn, and repeated in other parts of the garden, is the warm blue-mauve of *Aster × frikartii* 'Mönch' with bright pink diascias in front.

For a long time the aster family, Michaelmas daisies, suffered from an unfashionable reputation, whereas they are among the most indispensable autumn plants. Rather than mixed into a scheme for progression through the season, they are most effective grown *en masse*, where the ground can be given sufficient richness to guarantee great clumps of adjacent white, pink, blue, mauve and red.

Asters should be selected with care, not only to avoid those prone to mildew, but also to aim for an extended flowering season. Christopher Lloyd considers that 'by far the most rewarding is the lavender-coloured *Aster × frikartii* 'Mönch' which starts flowering in late summer and carries on for two months.' Perhaps Michaelmas daisies will see their favour restored to the degree with which they were regarded by Gertrude Jekyll in her own garden at Munstead Wood: 'They have, as they deserve to have, a garden to themselves. Passing along the wide path in front of the big flower border, and through the pergola that forms its continuation, with eye and brain full of rich, warm colouring of flower and leaf, it is a delightful surprise to pass through the pergola's right-hand opening and to come suddenly upon the Michaelmas Daisy garden in its full beauty ... the sight of a region where the flowers are fresh and newly opened, and in glad spring-like

profusion, when all else seems to be on the verge of death and decay, gives an impression of satisfying refreshment that is hardly to be equalled throughout the year.' As with much of her gardening, Miss Jekyll's Michaelmas daisy garden was hard work; the plants were dug up and replanted into freshly manured ground every year after flowering, using the best pieces of the old root with good clumps of crowns. They were staked in early summer with branching pea-sticks cut from her copse in winter. It is, however, possible to select Michaelmas daisies, such as 'Mönch' favoured, as we have seen, by both Christopher Lloyd and Penelope Hobhouse, and *Aster lateriflorus* 'Horizontalis', that can be divided less frequently – every two or three years – and which will stand without staking if sheltered by companion plants.

LEFT Michaelmas
daisies and sedums
form an ideal
autumn combination
for formal border
planting.

RIGHT In a parterre
bed at Barnsley the
autumn tints of
Deutzia scabra and
tall spires of acanthus
seedheads are set
against the freshness
of late-flowering
annual cosmos and
lobelia and white
*Leucanthemella
serotina.*

At Barnsley, the pinks and pinky reds of Michaelmas daisies are picked up by one of Rosemary Verey's early-autumn favourites: the annual cosmos, *Cosmos bipannatus*. The feathery leaves and mixed pink, pale red and sometimes white flowers, scattered through the denser plants in a border, add an airy lightness that autumn borders sometimes lack. In much of her garden at Barnsley a number of Rosemary Verey's choices for autumn flowering start contributing to the border earlier, when their young growth will accompany earlier summer-flowering plants, continuing the idea of 'layers in time' that have been evident since early spring (see page 20). This is especially true of the different lobelias that she recommends, one of the most striking of which, *Lobelia* 'Queen Victoria' has deep purple-red leaves followed by spires of bright crimson flowers. In many areas safeguarding these lobelias against the vagaries of winter weather can be combined with increasing their number by digging and potting up in late autumn the plants that have flowered and then, in spring, dividing into individual pots the crops of new small plants that have emerged, before planting them out after the danger of frost is past.

Rich, dark shades like those of the stately lobelias have become increasingly popular in the contemporary garden – nowhere more so that in Pam Lewis's garden at Sticky Wicket. Perhaps most representative is *Cosmos atrosanguineus*, with its peculiar scent of chocolate and a velvetiness to its dark purple-brown flowers that could only belong to autumn. She grows it with a complementary group of perennials that all produce intensely dark flowers at the same time of year: *Scabiosa atropurpurea*, *Angelica gigas* and *A. atropurpurea*, an almost black cornflower and the dark brown leaves of *Cimifuga simplex* 'Brunette'. Rich purple appears again among the mass of knautias that fill another bed.

Pam Lewis's aim is always to establish healthy colonies of perennial plant colonies, carefully grouped for colour – especially in the main round garden – that thereafter requiring little nurturing, and her gardening philosophy is exemplified at no better time of year than when summer passes into autumn. The garden's unbroken progress is especially due to self-sufficient plants – a

ABOVE Low sun brings out the fiery glow in this unusual combination of hemerocallis and the spinach-like red and golden orach (*Atriplex hortensis*).

RIGHT The increasingly feathery appearance of perennial grasses as they go to seed marks the transition from summer to autumn, while a stately yucca and late-flowering perennials maintain the flowering continuity.

pink/purple bed of the round garden is filled with sedums, eryngiums, astrantias, scabious and the unflatteringly named toad lily, *Tricyrtis formosana*, which has formed colonies to make a blanket of leaves beneath its multi-flowered stems.

Such permanent planting lies at the heart of Beth Chatto's garden, learnt by experience in the demanding conditions of the Essex coast. 'In this part of the country the garden in August is

often a sad sight, the grass burnt down, early plants finished and cut down, leaving perhaps weary-looking stands of mildewed phlox and Michaelmas daisies. If you do plenty of bedding out followed by copious watering the picture can be brighter, but I prefer more permanent planting … Walking along one of my dry sunny borders at this time of year, I enjoy stands of tall feathery bronze fennel above silver mounds of santolina, with Miss Willmott's ghost, *Eryngium giganteum*, seeded among them. Perhaps the loveliest of the sea hollies, she opens green, but slowly turns to a silver milky blue … I thought my first plant of *Calamintha nepetoides* was a dull little thing, but as summer fades into autumn these little plants produce more and more clouds of tiny pale blue flowers until they are a charming sight, crowded and humming with honey bees.' These are the subtly shifting and diminishing shades that one associates with the undisturbed passage of time in autumn – whether in the garden or the landscape beyond. They are quite different from the brilliant combinations at Hadspen or Great Dixter, but, as she goes on to demonstrate, Beth Chatto's garden has its own style of autumnal splendour: 'Round the corner of the house, below the west wall and on slightly better soil, is a surprising riot of rich growth. A purple-leaved vine is mixed up with trails of *Eccremocarpus scaber* whose burnt orange flowers are intertwined with the soft scarlet of the Cape figwort, *Phygelius capensis*. *Clematis tangutica* adds to the tangle, smothered with tiny lemon flowers, while bold contrast is made with the great white rumpled leaves of *Romneya coulteri*, the Californian tree poppy.'

In a way that typifies Beth Chatto's gardening skills, the plants she favours for this potentially testing time of year combine a number that are totally reliable and widely grown – astrantias and scabious, persicarias, penstemons, rudbeckias and Japanese anemones – with a selection of rarities that thrive with her because the conditions are comparable to their native ones. This is well illustrated by her descriptions of two plants originating from South Africa: the dainty *Schizostylis coccinea* 'Major', of which she says admiringly, 'Throughout autumn and mild days in winter,

LEFT *Kirengeshoma palmata*, a treasure of autumn's flowering palette, is best discovered in a shaded woodland corner.

FAR LEFT Seedheads and turning foliage suggest the changing season in this group, which includes *Stipa calamagrostis, Morina longifolia* and *Anthemis tinctoria* 'Wargrave'.

they open glistening shallow cups, jewel-like and cherry red', and the Cape hyacinth. 'Few plants in all the year can rival the elegant perfection of *Galtonia candicans*, the Cape Hyacinth … smooth stems (3–4ft tall) are topped with spires of pale green buds which slowly open to large ivory-white bells. Standing in drifts behind softly opened buds of *Sedum* 'Autumn Joy' providing a wax-textured, jade green foreground, they dispel the least hint of weariness in the garden scene.'

There is a similar sense of impact with a third exotic visitor, from Japan. *Kirengeshoma palmata* produces pale yellow flowers and demands warm, moist leafy soil in semi-shade, thereby suggesting it to be perfect for a woodland surprise. 'There is no plant in the garden to compare with this cool oriental beauty which keeps us waiting almost until the end of the flowering season before we can stand and wonder at its strange perfection,' she says. In many gardens statuary or other architectural ornament is used to make an unexpected statement, but for Beth Chatto, the whole charac-

ter of her garden suggests the use of plants rather than 'hardware' to surprise, and her use of a plant such as the kirengeshoma to achieve the same effect is entirely in keeping with the garden's overall philosophy.

The yellow bells of *Kirengeshoma palmata* bring a wonderful sense of fresh coolness to the garden at a time when the effect of many hot weeks is oppressive, and the same is true of shades of blue. Among the numerous salvias flowering in autumn is the unforgettable blue of *S. patens* and its paler form, 'Cambridge Blue'. Half-hardy, these salvias are unsatisfactory as perennials and much better (and very easily) grown as an annual from seed. Quantities of young plants can be put out in early June either as part of an autumn flowering scheme or to fill gaps that will be left as summer plants go over. They also mix ideally with their bright red shrubby relations such as *Salvia fulgens* and *S. greggii*.

These punctuation marks of colour are the decorative elements of the autumn garden for Beth Chatto, but the ethos of her garden revolves around the passage of time from summer through into winter, with plants whose changing form and habit will, without human interference, reflect and enhance this sense of progression. Some do not produce flower colour and for many that do this is secondary. In this light it is easy to appreciate the role that perennial grasses play in her garden, quite apart from the important element of bringing in a sense of the natural environment.

She grows many varieties suited to different situations, for instance the golden-tinted sedge *Carex elata* 'Aurea' and the variegated sword-like leaves of *Acorus calamus* 'Variegatus' close to the water's edge; various miscanthus in soil that does not dry out; and feathery *Stipa gigantea* and *Pennisetum villosum* in hot sunny places such as the gravel garden. They achieve height without requiring staking (of which she is not a devotee), but they also have much more to offer in myriad plant combinations. 'I love to see a few tall grasses such as *Stipa gigantea* rising high above the mounds and cushions of other perennial plants around them … Their fluttering ribbon-like leaves or glittering seedheads catch the sunlight or any passing movement of air. No other plant gives

ABOVE A hardy fuchsia,
F. 'Riccartonii', plays host to
Clematis viticella to give colour
and interest in a border right
through to the first frosts.

RIGHT As summer turns to
autumn, cannas, brugmansias,
phormiums and other exotics bring
a subtropical air to the old rose
garden at Great Dixter.

the same effect as grasses in the landscape, be they large and impressive, small and fluffy, or graceful and fountain-like.'

It is all these combined qualities, the gentle movement, the ability to be illuminated by low autumnal light, the increasingly autumn shades that conjure up images of stubble fields, and the manner in which grasses continue the autumn garden right into winter, that makes them so representative of the season. Like classic plants in other seasons – hellebores in spring, roses in summer – they immediately evoke a certain time of year as well as adding to their own form and textures an ability to make memorable plant combinations with their neighbours.

This capacity for being a 'good mixer' is an invaluable quality, one possessed by all the late-flowering clematis. Christopher Lloyd has described clematis as the perfect companion for summer roses (see page 32), and both Penelope Hobhouse and Rosemary Verey constantly emphasize the indispensability of the small-bloomed types that flower on through the autumn. They combine the achievement of continuity with plant combinations for earlier and later seasons, with their own delightful qualities of form and colour. These clematis are, as Penelope Hobhouse says, unfailingly adaptable: 'None of the small-flowered clematis is too flamboyant or attention-seeking, and they associate perfectly with other plants; they clothe high walls or tumble down low ones, mingle with other climbing vines without overrunning them and scramble through branches of deciduous trees and shrubs.' A minority of shrubs are at their best in autumn – caryopteris, it is true, provides a haze of powder blue and *Ceratostigma willmottianum* is spangled with its bright blue flowers until the first frosts, but many others have taken on a weary, dusty appearance that will not improve until the following spring. Any opportunity to cover or enliven them should be grasped, and they make ideal hosts for any of the late, small-flowered clematis species and their hybrids. The clematis will benefit from the natural frame a spring- or summer-flowering shrub provides and repay the compliment by giving new interest to its now dowdy branches.

Cut down in February or March they spring up each year to

twine their way through host plants or up trees, bearing copious quantities of flowers. One of the most delicate is 'Etoile Rose', with mottled pink-purple, nodding bell-shaped flowers; among the most vigorous is 'Huldine' with distinctive white flowers. Others that are outstanding are the Texensis 'Duchess of Albany' with pinky red pitcher-shaped flowers, the purple Viticellas 'Etoile Violette' and 'Minuet' (which Robin Lane Fox fell for after seeing it in Nancy Lancaster's garden at Haseley Court) and 'Alba Luxurians' whose pointed petals merge white and green.

C. viticella and *C. texensis* and their hybrids are usually in shades of crimson, purple and pink, but two other autumn clematis that are favourites of Rosemary Verey have yellow flowers. *Clematis rehderiana* carries clusters of pale primrose bells with a scent of cowslips, while *Clematis tangutica* is covered in brighter yellow

LEFT The falling leaves of
Acer japonicum contrast with the
year-round solidity of clipped yew
in a moment that captures the all
too transient glory of archetypical
autumn colour.

RIGHT Unforgettable delicacy and
colour characterize this partnership
of the autumn-flowering Texensis
clematis 'Etoile Rose' and the larger
flowered *C.* 'Perle d'Azur'.

lanterns that are replaced later in the year by silky seedheads that will remain all winter. Both are best grown as climbers into a host tree, the vigorous *C. tangutica* often reaching an impressive height.

Quite different from the clematis, but equally prized as an autumn-flowering climber, is the starry white-flowered *Solanum jasminoides* 'Album'. Rosemary Verey grows it in the courtyard at Barnsley and it is one of a select group of plants that Penelope Hobhouse includes in a small white area of her new garden in Dorset. It is not fully hardy everywhere, but protect a young plant until it establishes itself and it will then usually be safe from all but extreme frost and winter cold. Vigorous and best trained against a wall, it begins producing its superbly fresh white flowers in late summer, although autumn is its main season and the flowers continue to appear in quantity until the first frost.

Gertrude Jekyll approved of this plant and wrote glowingly of it in her neighbours' gardens:

'Its white clusters come into bloom in middle summer and persist till latest autumn. In two gardens near me it is of singular beauty; in the one case on the sunny wall of a sheltered court where it covers a considerable space, in the other against a high south retaining wall where, from the terrace above, the flowers are seen against the misty woodland of the middle distance and the pure grey-blue of the faraway hills.'

Exotic and showy by nature, *Solanum jasminoides* also fulfils what is an important priority for many gardeners during autumn – the provision of continuity from the last weeks of summer until the first frosts combine with dark mornings and afternoons to confirm the arrival of winter.

THE WINTER GARDEN

'TO THINK OF LEAF FALL AND THE ONSET OF

WINTER AS SAD IS ANTHROPOMORPHIC; THE

USUAL SILLY WAY WE HAVE AT LOOKING AT

THINGS FROM OUR OWN POINT OF VIEW.'

CHRISTOPHER LLOYD

A heavy fall of snow emphasizes
the pattern of the knot garden at
Barnsley, while the feathery shapes
of snow-covered bare branches in the
background provide a subtle contrast.

To regard winter as a time to be endured will condemn your garden to struggling mournfully from autumn round to spring. Instead it should be regarded as a season of duality, with its own planting fortes whose priorities and characteristics are unique, a time of vital, regenerative dormancy. Winter has a mood which should be respected, says Rosemary Verey: 'The countryside in winter is quiet, the light clear and the landscape uncluttered. The combinations and graduations of colour in a garden should reflect these months of repose.'

Winter planting's main priority is form and structure, both of the garden as a whole and relating to individual or groups of plants. The successful winter garden is one where this supersedes the plant association priorities of the rest of the year. What colours appear are decorative highlights against a background more constant than at any other time, as Rosemary Verey describes: 'Winter colour is nature's most sophisticated palette … the essential background colour is brown – turned earth, mulch, seeds, bark, catkins …' Against this canvas the shades of winter-flowering plants must be arranged so as to catch the low and watery sunlight and to open up corners of your garden that would be otherwise visually discarded for months. But more prominent will be the effect of those features in the garden with shape through the season: trees – whether deciduous or evergreen – shrubs and hedges.

To contemplate and plan your garden with these things foremost is not always easy; few gardeners actually think of the winter months first when devising either design or planting. It helps to remember that winter planting should both reflect the mood of the season – not try to make it something else – and reward those occasions when you arm yourself to fend off the elements and venture into the garden. As experienced gardeners emphasize time and again, those journeys from the house during winter should be made worthwhile with some trophy to take indoors. 'A winter corner should be a place, however small, where you can be sure of finding those special flowers that brave the weather,' says Rosemary Verey, 'and it should be tucked away so that you have a positive inducement to walk out of the house to enjoy your

choice of winter flowers.' While a winter garden should have highlights that can be admired from the warm sanctuary of indoors, Rosemary Verey's suggestion adds an element of discovery that is so rewarding at any time of the year.

The key is to understand that there is an inevitable simplicity compared to other seasons of the year – Roy Strong describes the appearance of his garden in winter as 'a church in Lent, stripped of its furnishings, so that one's eye falls back on the purity of the architecture, devoid of the distractions of ornament'. In a sense it is

ABOVE The burnished hues
and structural bareness of coloured
winter stems are immensely
evocative of the season. Here a
group of the most striking mix
together: *Rubus thibetanus*,
Cornus alba 'Kesselringii' and
Salix 'Erythroflexuosa'.

RIGHT The summer abundance of
the potager at Barnsley is replaced
by a picture of strong lines and
shapes, leeks bowing under a
covering of snow within their crisp
outline of clipped box hedges.

a two-dimensional simplicity. A border or flowerbed loses its body
and colour when the plants have died down for winter, but its
form can be retained by a tall hedge behind or low one in front
which also links it in to the surrounding areas. In a comparable
way the contribution of trees planted on a garden's edge changes;
in summer when covered in leaf they provide a dense boundary
but in winter their open shapes of bare branches will perhaps
frame a view that lasts for a few precious months.

Underlying all winter gardening must be an acceptance of the season's benefits as part of the annual cycle: 'It is a necessity, not just a necessary evil,' Christopher Lloyd emphasizes. 'You only have to see what a poor account of themselves roses give in the tropics (even at high altitudes) and how short-lived they are, to realize that without their winter, plants such as these burn themselves out. Others, which need cold in order to bring about the physiological changes that enable them to break dormancy in the following spring, are lost without it, remaining dormant for ever more.' So, carefully mulched borders and turned bare earth must be relished rather than tolerated. In her garden at Stone House Louisa Arbuthnott adheres to the long-established belief in 'putting the garden to bed': 'I would much rather admire the fashionable "frozen cobweb on dead twigs" look in someone else's garden and get far more satisfaction seeing everything cut down and heavily mulched ready for spring.'

Whether you cut down border perennials or leave the foliage to die off slowly is usually a matter of personal taste; doing the latter will perhaps encourage slugs but it will also help some half-hardy plants such as perennial grasses, penstemons or salvias to survive a mild winter. Either way, hand in hand with ground preparation during winter should be an assessment of your planting for different seasons – especially the peak of summer – and how it might be improved by changes. In this way winter's contribution to classic planting is indirect, by providing time for thoughtful analysis and the occasion for pruning, and for moving (or planning to move), splitting and replanting perennials that will improve planting in future seasons.

The idea of duality, the seasonal highlights combining with the preparation for the months ahead, allows the winter garden to come into its own so that although your level of activity will always have the practical limitations of few hours of daylight and regular interruptions by the weather, preparation for forthcoming seasons proceeds in an atmosphere of contentment. At the same

Tree shapes are given sharp emphasis in winter, their variety of outlines contributing to a garden's enduring framework.

time winter is when a garden is at its most open. With no leaf on deciduous trees or shrubs and only occasional height in borders and flowerbeds, the underlying design and structure is clearly revealed. What you see may be satisfying or it may suggest change and improvement, in which case this is the opportunity to act. Even when the ground is too hard to dig you will see where, for instance, a new bed or altering the shape of an existing one would be an improvement, where a new tree would cut out wind and provide some shade for plants which earlier in the year you have noticed suffering from the summer sun, or where a new path would enhance the planting in a border facing on to open lawn. None of these possible improvements would be so evident at any other time of year, nor is there the time to assess them as the rota of urgent jobs continues relentlessly.

Rosemary Verey is widely known as an inspired devotee of the winter garden, her passion coming initially through practising and observing in her own garden at Barnsley. Now in its maturity, the garden reveals the degree to which its winter appearance has played a role in the overall planning. She recommends winter as a particularly rewarding time to keep a gardening diary, because the quantity of flowering activity is sufficiently limited to be able to note it all. It is also the time when the notes recorded in previous weeks and months can be used either to effect or plan changes and additions to planting for peak times of the year.

The garden at Barnsley exemplifies the importance of evergreens during winter. 'Box edging can define borders, fastigiate junipers and cupressus create height and patterns,' comments Rosemary Verey. 'Almost everywhere in our garden are neatly clipped box balls and pyramids, usually to define the beginning or the end of a border, and there are standard golden privet and *Euonymus alatus* edging an otherwise characterless stone path.' While these plants all play a role throughout the year it is in winter that they are essentials. The rows of Irish yews (*Taxus baccata* 'Fastigiata') flanking the stone path from the house's garden door and extending across the lawn towards the boundary wall assume a memorable architectural quality at this time of year. The view

LEFT Looking
across the
architectural lines
of Barnsley's herb
garden towards the
yew walk is a
reminder of how
indispensable
clipped evergreens
are to the winter
garden.

RIGHT Clustered
berberis berries
are given great
intensity by a
covering of frost.

from the house along the lines of conical yews is also the perfect illustration of how winter is a season of dramatic changes in vistas and shapes. The focal point beyond the gate that leads from the main garden to the potager is a perfectly positioned silver birch (*Betula pendula*). Its dome of bare branches stands silhouetted against the skyline, the trees of an ancient hedgerow continuing the theme of silhouette on the far boundary of the adjoining meadow, and the progression from the house along the yew walk to the birch and view beyond encapsulates a bond between garden and landscape that does not exist at other times of the year.

The yew walks lead to one of the garden's main junctions where, again, the well-planned choice of trees for a key position comes into its own in winter. In line with the yews are a pair of weeping cherries, *Prunus* × *yedoensis* 'Shidare-yoshino', whose branches cascade to the ground like overflowing glasses. These

two trees are positioned at right angles, so they lead into the lime walk, in winter one of the garden's most spectacular structural features. The tightly clipped branches of the lime are surmounted by the bright scarlet new growth which gives it its name: *Tilia platyphyllos* 'Rubra,' red-twigged lime. The vista continues from the lime walk straight into the laburnum walk, whose winter canopy of branches twisted together Rosemary Verey describes as 'tracery'. The continuing strength of shape as one passes from the

limes on either side to the laburnums overhead, allied with the subtle shift in emphasis and colour shades of brown, combine to give an effect that is quite lost in other seasons with the softening cover of leaf and the distraction of flower colour.

These areas of the garden demonstrate the strong impact that the bare branches of deciduous trees can have. Elsewhere, well-sited standards give their varying form to otherwise open views and, Rosemary Verey stresses, it is the time of year when their shape — fastigiate, cup-shaped, pendulous or round — is especially noticeable. The other crucial element in the garden's winter form is the use of evergreens, whether clipped into topiary or left to make their natural shapes. Yew and box (*Buxus sempervirens*) are undoubtedly the best evergreens for topiary, making such strong shapes in winter, as well as for hedges that sustain a garden's framework. Rosemary Verey points out that low box edging the front of a border along grass or beside a paved path assumes its boldest impact during winter, when her garden's visual effect is primarily one of lines and forms rather than colours. Outside one door of the house the horizontal diamond pattern of clipped box in the herb garden makes a dramatic contrast with the columnar, vertical lines of the Irish yews that break the skyline in the background.

It is similarly true of the knot garden beneath one side of the house at Barnsley, where Rosemary Verey admires the 'neat, disciplined three-dimensional strapwork, the perfect embellishment for any garden in winter'. She recommends a pattern of box and wall germander infilled with gravel, with a higher clipped evergreen bush to make a central feature (*Phillyrea angustifolia* at Barnsley). The formalized pattern of a knot garden, at its crispest during winter, requires careful integration into a garden's overall scheme. At Barnsley it has an ideal setting adjacent to the house, where its geometric shapes associate well with the house's architecture, but it would be equally at home in a scheme where the architectural lines of hedges, paths and lawn predominate.

Such a stylized planting design is not to everyone's taste, and for evergreen form that is suitable to a wide variety of garden situations there are other candidates to extend the garden's range of winter planting. 'Two greens I am always grateful for in winter,' says Rosemary Verey, 'are the shiny texture of *Choisya ternata* and the leathery feel of *Osmanthus delavayi.*' She also uses the evergreen holm oak, *Quercus ilex,* and *Euonymus fortunei,* both of which are ideally suited to clipping into neat shapes, as well as the variegated holly, *Ilex × altaclerensis* 'Golden King' which has butter yellow edging to its slightly rounded leaves. Even such a brief selection as this illustrates how the appreciation and perception of evergreens has developed. Only twenty or thirty years ago the most popular use of evergreens in the winter garden was conifers to provide contrast and background to a carpet of winter heathers, tall cypresses or flattened, prostrate junipers matching the muddy mauves of the heather for gloominess.

The framework that the trees and hedges give to the garden at Barnsley sustain it throughout winter's cycle. But they also provide the backdrop for the small-scale but bright decoration that often appears shortly after Christmas – the first cyclamens, to be followed by snowdrops and other little bulbs braving the weather. Whether in the grass beneath the trees of the wilderness, around the trunks of apples in the potager, or scattered through the main garden's various borders, they provide the visual encouragement that takes the garden into early spring.

Rosemary Verey is not the only gardener to emphasize the degree to which the winter garden is predominantly part of nature, rather than fully controlled by man. Of Great Dixter, Christopher Lloyd says; 'I love my winter garden because of its silence and emptiness; the slow pace, not dead, not even merely ticking over – there is always a forward impulse – but a gentle stirring. Even when the weather is rough there is a feeling throughout of inner calm.' Without the distraction of plants, he says, there is time to enjoy the garden birds and to admire peculiarities such as the black berries of Christmas box (*Sarcococca confusa*) which at a busier time of the year would be overshadowed by something else. In the old kitchen garden at Great Dixter the yew hedges that enclose and divide the area assume their greatest prominence, complementing the architectural shapes of the

house's skyline, while in the long mixed border and other parts of the garden trunks of trees, solid shapes of evergreen shrubs and stands of grasses and bamboo bind the picture together.

Penelope Hobhouse is another gardener who feels that winter combines its seasonal quality with a vital role in the garden's inevitable annual change: 'A garden plan is not like an architectural blueprint, it can and must be revised as the garden is planted and begins literally to grow. It is not only the planning, planting and anticipation that makes gardening enthralling, there is also the pleasure of changing and adjusting as the expected or unexpected happens. Watching a garden grow and having to adapt it each year makes gardening endlessly interesting. Next year can always be different and better.'

At Tintinhull the garden's walls and hedges creating the different enclosures give the garden an immediate structure most evident

The ability of grasses to maintain their shape makes a great feature of the winter garden, as with these massed clumps of frost-covered miscanthus and pennisetum, with phormium and artemisia.

during winter. As the dense planting that predominates in other seasons disappears the architectural qualities, the classical symmetry of line, come into their own. At the same time, some areas of the garden have always been consciously planted for winter effect, most especially Eagle Court, a walled area closest to one side of the house. Here, winter-flowering evergreens demonstrate their importance, whether in their own right or as the background to flowering perennials, and interest is retained throughout the year by structural evergreens – as at Barnsley the formality of the planting complemented by the house's architecture. The backbone of the court is formed by four pairs of clipped box domes along the central stone path that leads from the house terrace out to the other areas of garden beyond. The planting is in beds around two rectangles of grass on either side of the path. Of the overall effect Penelope Hobhouse has written, 'Although the

perimeter borders appear to be planted informally, in fact there is repetition of blocks of shapes and colours, very much in Phyllis Reiss's style and conveying a strong design message … For me, in designing for others and now in creating beds of my own at Bettiscombe, repetition without exact symmetry seems to provide an essential key.'

Phyllis Reiss laid out the garden at Tintinhull in the 1940s, and some plants survive from her original scheme, including a now magnificent *Mahonia japonica*, and a companion planting of evergreen *Choisya ternata* and *Corylopsis pauciflora* in two corners. The choisya's white spring flowers are preceded by the racemes of lightly scented yellow flowers of the deciduous corylopsis. Another evergreen shrub that is a strong winter feature in the court is *Itea ilicifolia*, its arching stems clothed in glossy green leaves, subtly enhanced every autumn by tassels of lime green florets.

Among the plants that Penelope Hobhouse added were euphorbias, not least for 'their blue-green linear foliage in winter' and the early spring-flowering climber, *Stauntonia hexaphylla*. Foliage in winter spreads to a selection of perennials that keep their leaves, including bergenias, hellebores and epimediums. Penelope Hobhouse's conclusion on the planting's success is that there may be no warm or bright flower colour, 'instead strong accents are provided by plant shapes and good foliage which extend through all the seasons.' At no time of year are they more prominent than during winter.

At Bettiscombe, Penelope Hobhouse's new garden in Dorset, it is intriguing to see how clipped evergreens again form part of the fundamental framework of her design. The architectural quality of shaped evergreens, especially evident in winter, is sufficiently strong to link a whole area together, an effect that can be seen with Barnsley's avenue of Irish yews and, with interesting differences, in the repeating shapes of the yew topiary at Great Dixter. At Bettiscombe, symmetrically placed glass doors on opposite sides of the house open on to avenues of yew pillars, on one side forming a backbone into the meadow garden that links the house with the countryside and Dorset hills to the north and on the other making a similar bond with the square walled garden to the south. It is in winter that the effect of this symmetry is most striking, described by Penelope House as 'this repetition in the inner and outer gardens linking the high-walled *hortus conclusus* with the orchard and the landscape.'

Beth Chatto is similarly conscious of the bond between garden and landscape that can be opened up in winter and presented in

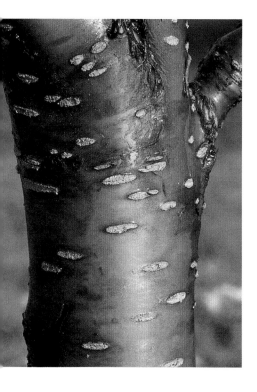

LEFT The bark of many trees in the cherry family, such as this *Prunus maackii* 'Amber Beauty', has a rich, warm shine best appreciated in winter.

RIGHT The translucent seedheads of honesty (*Lunaria annua*) and the lingering colour of sedum behind characterize the transition from autumn into the depths of winter.

the simplest but most rewarding manner. She describes a white-barked birch, *Betula utilis jacquemontii*, that stands sentinel on her open lawn: 'On a dark winter afternoon my eye is caught by its perfect shape, a delicate ivory fan outlined against the black bulk of holly that stands some way beyond it. My tree stands alone in mown grass, reflecting itself like a swan in a small, dark-surfaced pool.' It catches the smallest flicker of low winter sunlight, and in extreme cold the white of the birch's bark becomes truly luminous. Planted in open lawn like this, or on a boundary with fields beyond, as at Barnsley, the ghostly silhouette that is the outstand-

ing characteristic of silver and white-barked birches is even more arresting than when growing naturally in deciduous woodland.

In the light of her philosophy of developing permanent plant communities that have a large element of self-sufficiency throughout the year, an equally important aspect of Beth Chatto's garden in winter is the appearance of the main planted areas such as the gravel garden. In a garden of more formal style and character, the idea of cutting down and tidying for winter – 'putting the garden to bed' as Louisa Arbuthnott does – has a curious formality of its own. But the contrasting outlook enjoys the idea of winter as a period of decay and renewal. The visible changes have their own fascination, producing lingering foliage, seedheads and arched stems brittle with frost. Perennial grasses, which retain their graceful stems, are most representative of classic planting for the contemporary garden in winter. They provide rare movement against the blocks of evergreens or bare deciduous branches, and whether in a border or wilder setting, immediately bring a sense of the natural landscape into the garden.

Foliage that takes on interesting coloration through the winter months is a special asset. Beth Chatto relishes the brownish purple hue of bergenias, and recollects the effect in her garden of *Persicaria affinis*: 'With the onset of winter and frosty nights, the leaves do not drop off, but remaining shapely; they turn deep reddish brown, a lovely lively colour, making a vivid contrast with the emerald green mown grass when lit by winter sunlight.' Even more brilliant is the foliage of *Sedum spurium* 'Atropurpureum', whose foliage she considers 'so alluring it hardly needs the rose red flowers'.

Beth Chatto enjoys those grasses and perennial foliage whose contribution to the winter garden is part of the year's cycle, but she is equally aware of the potential for winter-flowering plants. Talking about witch hazel, *Hamamelis mollis*, she points out that planting it with a protective evergreen background close by will not only show off the spidery yellow flowers to best effect, but also slightly warm the air to encourage the scent. Hybridizing between the Japanese *Hamamelis japonica* and the Chinese *Hamamelis mollis* has led to the development of coppery red flowers, but the original *H. mollis* or the paler *H.* × *intermedia* 'Pallida' remain the most generally recommended.

Hamamelis are one of the select group of winter-flowering shrubs treasured for their deliciously scented flowers produced on still-bare branches, a quality shared by the winter-flowering viburnums, especially *Viburnum farreri* (syn. *fragrans*) and *Viburnum* × *bodnantense* 'Dawn', and the wintersweet, *Chimonanthus praecox*. Pam Lewis so enjoys their scent wafting on a crisp day that at Sticky Wicket she plants them under the windows. Rosemary

Verey, in contrast, prefers their pinpoint flowers to light up the winter landscape and finds them most effective when seen from a distance. She also makes the point that their foliage is uninteresting – in a hot, dry summer not only dull but unsightly – and so they are better positioned to entice you into the garden. She finds them 'wonderful plants for the wild garden and also for a shrub border, where you can use them as host plants for summer-flowering clematis.'

The white or pink-flushed flower heads of viburnums and the waxy yellow of wintersweet are undeniably charming, although their scent is their prime feature, but for intensity of both flower colour and scent, daphnes win on both counts. Some, such as

Winter-flowering shrubs provide a range of scents whose richness dispels the seasonal bleakness. Witch hazels and viburnums are two of the best, notably *Hamemelis* × *intermedia* 'Sunburst' (left) and *Viburnum* × *bodnantense* 'Dawn'.

Daphne mezereum, are deciduous and flower on bare wood; but the great advantage of the evergreen varieties is their compact, domed shape, which makes them ideal for giving both structure and winter interest to a border group. Daphnes flower from mid-winter through to late spring and one of the earliest to flower, *Daphne odora* 'Aureomarginata', is also one of the most reliably hardy and the strongest scented. Rosemary Verey grows it on the

LEFT The gentle texture and colour
of *Iris unguicularis* seem to defy even
the harshest of winter conditions
and, like many other of the season's
best plants, they are ideal for picking
and bringing into the house.

RIGHT The eerie white of
Rubus biflorus stands out like a ghost
in front of the wine red stems of
Salix alba vitellina 'Britzensis'.

terrace next to the house at Barnsley, where its scent is immediately enjoyable and its neat shape fits into the architectural setting.

Quite different in character, but also ideally suited to being planted against the house, is arguably the most rewarding winter flowerer, the perennial *Iris unguicularis*. For Beth Chatto it is 'on my list of top ten garden plants.' In poor stony soil that remains dry, it forms dense clumps of grassy leaves and, well protected in a dry sunny corner against the house wall, it will often flower before Christmas. The pencil-thin, soft mauve flowers have exquisitely rolled petals and should be picked as buds, to open in a vase of water. The form 'Walter Butt' has pale lavender flowers of even great delicacy but in either case few flowers so capture the beguiling combination of fragility and warmth that sums up the winter garden.

The texture and colour of these little irises is reassuringly soft, but there can be intensity in winter colour, too, typified by the brilliance of some barks. Contrasting with the delicate, cold beauty of white-barked or silver birches in Beth Chatto's garden are the glowing shades of russet-barked *Prunus serrula* whose fleeting, uninteresting flowers in spring are more than compensated for at this time of year. It is a tree for the wild or meadow garden, where bulbs will appear in long grass later in the year and where its best companions are stronger-flowering blossom trees. Equally warm-looking is the cinnamon-barked strawberry tree, *Arbutus* × *andrachnoides*, with evergreen leaves and clusters of pendulous white flowers that are followed in late autumn by the distinctive red fruits from which it gets its name (but not its taste – arbutus 'strawberries' are mouth-puckeringly bitter). It is best suited to a sheltered position in front of a wall or hedge, its shape and foliage providing a background to planting. For a standard tree on a lawn, the acers or maples combine winter shape with a variety of striking barks – snakebarks, such as *Acer davidii*; the brown papery *Acer griseum* that flakes off its old layers to reveal a brighter one beneath; or the pinky red hue of *Acer palmatum* 'Sango-kaku'.

We have already seen the startling effect of the burnished new growth of the red-twigged limes in Rosemary Verey's garden. Perhaps the most vivid winter colours, bright and yet cold, are provided by the young stems – red, orange and yellow – of dogwoods (*Cornus alba*, *stolonifera* and *sanguinea*) and willows (*Salix* spp.). Penelope Hobhouse considers that these coloured willows look most effective beside water (where they enjoy the moist conditions), their clusters of bright stems ideal to punctuate the openness of the winter landscape. The same effect is achieved by planting them along a garden boundary, in a wild garden or in a woodland clearing. An important point when planting dogwoods and willows for the effect of their coloured stems is that they should be as massed as possible. One *Cornus alba* can be a sorry sight, but the other extreme is exhilarating: a whole bank of brilliant red to be revealed from a distance, glowing in the winter landscape like a hot coal in ash.

More easily integrated into a border planting scheme are the arching white stems of *Rubus thibetanus* or *R. biflorus*, related to the bramble. Less widely grown but preferred by Rosemary Verey are the stems of *Rubus phoenicolasius* and *R. cockburnianus*. While

these showy brambles take on their winter hues without any encouragement, the dogwoods and willows are most spectacular if cut back in spring every two years, to spur them into producing more, and more brilliantly coloured, young wands.

Seen from a distance, whether against a grim steely sky, illuminated by low afternoon sunlight, or shimmering with frost, these glowing stems embody the stark balance of brightness and cold that is such a part of winter and should be reflected in the season's planting. They have the permanence that the winter garden requires to hold its own against the openness that appears with the loss of foliage; they are enhanced by the clarity of the season's light; and they hold the promise of regeneration, for they are the young growth that in the coming seasons will be adorned with foliage and take the garden to the next stage of the yearly cycle.

CREATING FORMALITY

'YOU CAN INTRODUCE FORMAL ACCENTS
EVEN IN THE MOST INFORMAL HERBACEOUS
BORDERS, MERELY, FOR EXAMPLE, BY SITING
CLUMPS OF ONE PROMINENT PERENNIAL
EQUIDISTANT FROM ANOTHER.'

ROY STRONG

Here, formality is achieved as much
by the detail and arrangement of the
planting as by the more traditional
means of confinement within a border
of overall regular shape. Regular
progressions of colour and of the
heights of adjacent groups of plants
both give an idea of formality
introduced rather than imposed.

For many gardeners the idea of formality in planting immediately suggests restrictions, regimented shapes and lines that dictate a garden's nature and appearance in an overbearing and artificial manner, not allowing for any sense of naturalness. The theme of this chapter, however, follows Roy Strong's observation, that formality in the contemporary garden can be introduced in a surprising number of ways, some of them visually dominant, others no more than the most subtle suggestion. One area of a large garden might be formalized by the use of permanent structural plants (most usually clipped hedges), in the way that plants are grouped and associated, in the use of an

existing structure of garden walls, in the introduction of ornament or, as we shall see in the next chapter, with the use of water. To use one simple example of how a note of formality can be introduced to planting, a late-summer clematis clambering unchecked through an evergreen shrub gives a sense of natural informality, whereas to train the same clematis up a wooden or metal support immediately introduces an element of formality.

One of the most significant developments of the contemporary garden is to diminish the long-accepted boundaries between formality and informality – the former traditionally provided by structure, the latter by plants – by using plants of formal habit or in certain combinations so as to introduce formality into the most relaxed scheme. No visitor to Beth Chatto's garden would leave with an impression of formality, yet in the broad sweep of border at the entrance the bold groups of bergenias, whose lush foliage is evergreen year-round, provide an instant sense of structure and definition. And the leylandii hedge was planted behind the border not only to provide shelter but because, as Beth Chatto explains, 'this hedge is the nearest approach I have to an architectural wall'. Beth Chatto's entrance border also demonstrates how repetition of colour and form gives a sense of unified structure and symmetry. The repeat bright yellow flowers of achilleas, the silvery hue of eryngiums – as well as their clearly defined forms – and the greens of euphorbias in varying heights – *E. characias wulfenii*, *E. polychroma* and *E. dulcis* – all give the planting a well-ordered appearance that is far from haphazard.

Here and in other areas of her garden Beth Chatto has demonstrated that by planting in clearly thought-out groups formal

LEFT Even in a cottage garden, with mixed aquilegias rambling in the foreground, the architectural shape of a golden conifer gives a suggestion of formality - as does the bold foliage of a cardoon behind the bench.

RIGHT Architectural form is the primary feature in this group of grasses and grass-like foliage – *Molinia caerulea* 'Variegata', *Carex elata* 'Aurea' and *Iris pseudacorus* – in front of *Physocarpus opulifolius* 'Luteus'.

RIGHT Looking along the divided border on one side of the central lawn at Bourton House, the manner in which the waves of *Alchemilla mollis* roll along the front of the borders ties the planting together with a rhythmic sense of movement.

unity is introduced to even the most varied of associations. 'I may plant a tall feathery fennel. Beside the fennel might be the shrub *Phlomis fruticosa*, a bulky rounded shrub. As strong contrast in form you might use a spiky-leaved yucca nearby and then the eye will travel down to low mounds of ballota or santolina, and finally descend to the mat plants. Together they form a related group. If you can compose individual groups linked together within the external frame it makes the planting look more interesting both overall and in detail.' This is where plant association can change the accepted perception of formality in the garden and broaden the scope. It is far removed from old-fashioned formal styles such as a geometric rose garden, and instead focuses upon the conscious arrangement of harmonious plant neighbours to create a unified composition.

This is perhaps formality at its most subtle – or informal. In most instances a formal planting is achieved by simpler means, notably by the use of evergreens and by the repeat use of single-colour flowering plants. It is interesting to think of the possible variations: a border with a catholic range of colours and shapes, with plants spilling out of the front over adjoining lawn or path, has a nicely carefree but potentially disorganized appearance. By introducing a

LEFT Formality through a predominant colour scheme: in this planting detail 'Iceberg' roses are married with the silver foliage of artemisias and onopordums.

RIGHT A geometric pattern of clipped hedges and topiary in Roy Strong's garden, The Laskett: flowers here play a much reduced role and its symmetry remains constant year-round.

predominance – or even the exclusive use – of one plant, such as *Alchemilla mollis*, all along the front, a strong note of unity is introduced to the planting. The formality becomes stronger and more architectural if, instead of alchemilla, the front of the border is contained with a low hedge of either lavender or clipped box.

It is important to appreciate how the application of formality to planting in different ways can give rise to greatly varied effects. The use of a single colour produces a veneer of formality within which there can be considerable variety in the types of plants used and their habits. Vita Sackville-West demonstrated this most famously in her white garden at Sissinghurst; shrub roses, white-flowered perennials and herbs, as well as climbing and rambling plants are bound together by the colour theme and the garden's structure of clipped box hedges. White is a popular colour for such a scheme but perhaps the simplest theme is where the predominant colour is green. Take, for example, a shady path lined on both sides by clumps of hostas. The symmetry of the foliage shapes and

sizes and the interwoven shades of green from yellowy lime to deep glaucous blue are given formality by the very simplicity of the planting and the limited, but far from boring, palette.

Neither of the gardens at Hadspen House in Somerset or Sticky Wicket in Dorset is formal in the conventional sense of the word. But in certain areas, notably in the main curving flower border in the walled garden at Hadspen and in the round garden at Sticky Wicket, the deliberate arrangement of colour in progressive shades presents an unquestionably formal scene. As at Sissinghurst, the underlying orderliness allows for great variety in the planting detail which can be enjoyed up close; when viewed from a distance the overall effect is one of consummate harmony, of unbroken progression from one group of plants to the next.

Over and above such formality produced by the details of plant combinations, there are – and will always be – many gardens where the dominant style is truly formal. These have their origins in the parterres and knot gardens of centuries past. Whatever plants are used, they are contained within a pattern of geometric shapes, and the garden is built up around a framework of axial paths, trees or shrubs planted in straight lines to form allées or avenues. Where there are changes of level these are formalized into terraces with flights of steps and where divisions are required they are provided by walls or clipped hedges. Such gardens have a reassuring sense of orderliness. If built up with a structure of evergreens they have a year-round permanence with no reliance upon seasonal flowering for short-term effect. They are also well-suited to a garden on the smallest scale. A pattern of box-hedged squares infilled with flowers in two or three primary colours combines formality of structure and planting and is ideal for seasonal

changes from spring bulbs to summer annuals. Such spatially con-fined formality will immediately fit comfortably into the smallest area or make a self-contained formal element within a larger garden. And, as gardeners rediscover down the centuries, formality can offset the architecture of a house to best effect and establish permanent visible links between the house and its garden.

Rosemary Verey's garden at Barnsley illustrates this idea with three formal statements that all bind the house and garden together. The first, and most important structurally, is the yew walk, a paved path lined by pairs of Irish yews that leads from the house's drawing room door across the garden towards an opening in the boundary wall on the far side. The second is the herb

LEFT Columnar Irish yews underplanted primarily with mixed helianthemums line the flagged path across the lawn of Barnsley House's parterre garden. The combination of planting and the axial vista bind house and garden together.

RIGHT Apple blossom and clipped box create a planting framework around the paths in Rosemary Verey's potager.

garden, leading away from the kitchen door and parallel to the yews, a long rectangle of clipped box hedges making a pattern of diamond beds infilled with herbs. The herb garden's formal layout is ideally suited to its position. In one direction, from the house, it edges the path leading into the garden and at the same time makes a neat statement in front of the boundary hedge to one side. Equally important, the formal pattern of the clipped box is prominent whether in winter, when it is mainly structural, and in summer, when the little hedges contain the green, silver and variegated tapestry of herb foliage.

The third formal element is the knot garden on the other side of the house, facing south across the garden. Laid out in front of a castellated veranda, the knot garden is a permanent pattern of clipped box in two varieties, *Buxus sempervirens* 'Suffruticosa' and *B. sempervirens* 'Aureomarginata', and germander, *Teucrium* × *lucidrys*, with clipped evergreen hollies on the four corners. The whole composition is an ideal complement to the architectural pattern of the house behind. On achieving the intended effect, Rosemary Verey has commented that: 'As Humphry Repton recommended two centuries ago, any planting close to a house helps to keep it anchored into its surroundings. Our knots have become almost a shadow of the house.'

These three design elements of the garden at Barnsley are all structural and permanent. But Rosemary Verey's planting also illustrates occasions where the introduction of formality is most suitable when thematic rather than stylistic. Helianthemums (rock roses) are cheerfully informal, but planted along the path of the yew walk, their bright shades of magenta, red, orange, yellow and white spreading out across the paving stones in early summer, they are lent a formality from their sheer mass and by their association with the yews – a formality not of style but of theme.

Similarly, the strong axis of the yew walk across the lawn in front of the house suggested the formal pattern of four symmetrically shaped beds that, with openings between, enclose the lawn. Once formality is established in the structure, it can disappear in the style of planting. 'When Gertrude Jekyll wrote that a garden should curtsey to the house,' explains Rosemary Verey, 'I think she meant that it should be in harmony, in keeping with the style of the house, but should not outshine it in any way. Our lawn with its four flanking beds, I hope, does just this … Each of their shapes is almost identical, and each fulfils my criterion of putting on a continuous display of planting through all the seasons, but

LEFT The combination of clipped yew hedging and stone ornament gives an immediate atmosphere of formality that adjacent planting softens and complements.

RIGHT This view of the Eagle Court at Tintinhull shows how the enclosure, with its domes of clipped box along the central path, provides the ideal link between the classical house and terrace and the vista through the further garden areas beyond.

that is where their similarity ends. Each of the beds has its own distinct planting character and colour scheme, linked by the thread of my own thoughts which runs through them all.'

The formality of this area that is integrally linked to the house is in the structure, to provide harmony between house and garden and a framework for planting, illustrating Rosemary Verey's ideal of 'strong design softened by an exuberance of planting'. Elsewhere in the garden at Barnsley formal planting takes on a more definite role. An axial walk of pleached limes leads straight into a

laburnum tunnel with seasonal underplanting. The pleached red-twigged limes (*Tilia platyphyllos* 'Rubra') retain their neat symmetry throughout the year, whether covered in fresh green foliage in summer, or in winter when their tightly clipped branches are adorned with a canopy of bright red twigs. The underplanting is limited to a few small early plants including species crocuses, anemones and cyclamens. In the laburnum walk the architectural effect of the trained tunnel of branches is complemented in early summer when the yellow racemes of the laburnum mix with mauve wisteria and the rounded heads of *Allium hollandicum* stretch up below. But both before and after this summery scene, the underplanting is given formality by a restricted colour scheme, first with bright red tulips and later, after the alliums, by a rich green carpet of hostas. Another ingredient in the scheme is the symmetry of form that comes from repeating the same plants; the tulip and allium stems topped with first red and then mauve flowers stretching up towards the canopy above and later the green carpet of the hostas.

Penelope Hobhouse considers that her fifteen years at Tintinhull had the most profound influence on her gardening work and it was in that garden that she explored the balance of structure and planting, adding her own individuality to the legacy of her predecessor Phyllis Reiss who created the garden. Tintinhull was laid out in the style of the garden at Hidcote, which Phyllis Reiss knew well and acknowledged to be the main influence on her work. Its essential character is formal, reflecting the proximity to the classical house; its arrangement in adjoining geometric enclosures or 'rooms'.

Penelope Hobhouse's philosophy of 'formality and profusion' that Tintinhull instilled is similar in aspiration to Rosemary Verey's ideal of 'strong design and exuberant planting'. Equally important, the planting of the garden's different enclosed 'rooms', while clearly having the scope for individuality, required at least a sense of orderliness, if not exact formality in their compositions. 'Working in Phyllis Reiss's garden,' she says, 'I have absorbed her sense of scale and structure and learned the importance of repetition in

planting to prevent the restlessness produced by too much variety.' She found that working in a garden with a long-established and architectural framework produced an overall unity and feel of movement through the garden that actively encouraged varied treatment of the adjoining compartments – the impact of the variety being increased by the element of discovery as a new area is revealed. Within each compartment the individual character had to be firmly defined, the emphasis on repetition rather than endless variety resulting in a harmonious but not strained formality.

It is interesting to see how this is achieved in different areas. The Eagle Court lies immediately beyond the terrace in front of the main classical facade of the house, and its treatment always demanded formality so that, as at Barnsley, 'it has a symmetry that balances the architecture.' The basis of the formality is the repetition of structural plants: domes of clipped box along the central path; mirror clumps of rosemary on the corners of the borders and the path, and in the borders great clumps of euphorbias and evergreen shrubs such as sarcococcas and choisyas which give

year-round structure. There is also a balance in the flower colour of shrubs, climbers and perennials, with a strong presence of blue, mauve and purple. In the two halves of the court, dissected by the central path, the symmetry extends from being primarily architectural into the detail of the planting, with repeated clumps of Hidcote lavender, blue agapanthus, purple *Verbena bonariensis* and late-summer anemones.

The composition of Tintinhull's fountain garden is based on formality of both design and planting. The axial view across the lily pool leads through the white garden (where pink rods of *Dierama pulcherrimum*, just visible, add a note of variety), to the smaller area beyond filled with symmetrical groups of mainly variegated foliage.

In the fountain garden the central area around the fountain pool is formalized by its one-colour flowering scheme and continues in the same vein into the two small adjacent areas. The whole ensemble is enclosed by yew hedges with central openings on all four sides leading to a circle of paving around the pool and in response, as Penelope Hobhouse describes, 'the planting is quite formal with repetitive, rather than mirror-image, groups of silver- and grey-leaved plants with white or pale flowers.' Within the beds 'Iceberg' roses in front and clipped standard silver-leaved willows in the back corner of each bed, set off by clipped yew behind, are the primary structural plants. Equally prominent is the symmetrical effect of the pairs of ornamental crab apples, *Malus* 'John Downie' on one side and *M. tschonoskii* on the other, that flank the paths just outside the yew hedges to north and south.

Harking back to the point made about the white garden at Sissinghurst, where the formality of the colour scheme allows for variations in the planting, Penelope Hobhouse stresses that this variation is also made necessary by varying conditions. In a scheme where the aim is mirrored or repeat planting, careful choice of plants is crucial to gain the same effect in two contrasting situations, where one bed, for instance, may be largely shaded and its 'twin' drier and sunny. Here, creamy-flowered *Primula* 'Lady Greer' thrives in a damp shady corner, while *Lysimachia ephemerum* is equally happy in a spot of nearly full sun. Perhaps most effective is the way the white and cream theme unfolds through the year: from 'Purissima' tulips to irises (their vertical shapes ideal for punctuating the corners of bed), honesty (*Lunaria annua*) and stocks (*Malcolmia maritima*), white delphiniums and *Lychnis coronaria*, late-summer *Anemone* × *hybrida* (syn. *japonica*) and white colchicums in autumn.

Although it is called the white garden, ever since Phyllis Reiss's day the colour has not been ruthlessly imposed and one of the most deft touches is the inclusion in the layout of two small rectangular beds set in the paving and facing each other across the pool. In late summer clumps of white-flowered agapanthus flourishing here are overhung by the draping stems of pink-flowered angel's fishing rods, *Dierama pulcherrimum*. The mixture of colour shades in the white garden, ranging from creamy yellow to pink, illustrate that white or other single-colour planting schemes are usually shown to best effect when a small degree of associated colour contrast is introduced. A white garden planted only with, for example, 'Blanc Double de Coubert' roses, philadelphus, white stocks and phloxes, would benefit from the subtle introduction of variety, which would emphasize rather than compromise the whiteness of the colour scheme.

To one side of the white garden is a small rectangle of two beds divided by a central path and backed by yew hedges. Here the architectural formality that can be achieved with certain plants is memorably displayed. The two 'stars' are a pair of *Cornus controversa* 'Variegata', whose layers of branches and creamy green leaves have been rightly compared to a wedding cake. Their natural symmetry is enhanced by their mirror positioning and their impact heightened by the predominantly foliage planting in the beds below – principally hostas, but including rodgersias and Scotch thistles (*Onopordum acanthium*).

On the other side of the white garden colour formality is extended into the azalea beds, where the principal colours are yellow and gold. This combination involves both flower and foliage colour: the yellow of azaleas, Welsh poppies (*Meconopsis cambrica*) and lilies, and the golden foliage of *Philadelphus coronarius* 'Aureus'. The rich effect is cooled by repeat planting of hostas at intervals along the border front and set off by the clipped yew hedges behind.

Tintinhull demonstrates how formality can be extended from a garden's permanent structure into the detail of planting in a way that is immensely harmonious. At Arley Hall in Cheshire, the garden is an interesting example of how long-established formal features hugely increase the sense of scale and visual impact. An avenue of evergreen oaks, *Quercus ilex*, clipped into towering cylinders, is a monochrome statement in its own right, but the formality achieved by Arley's double herbaceous borders is more disguised. Extending for over 100 m (300 ft) on either side of a

generously wide expanse of lawn, the deep borders lead to an heroically proportioned ornamental seat at the far end. There is a formality of plant architecture in the use of clipped yew not only as backing hedges but making scrolling buttresses that repeat a rhythm along the borders like pillars along a house.

But the impact is given its most interesting dimension by the detailed planting of the borders, in the associations and repetitions of the plants themselves. While they are not consciously mirror imaged – they are too large – there is a repeat symmetry both across the central lawn from one border to another, and in the progression along each from one yew-divided section to the next, which produces a supremely elegant formality of style. In a sense

it is a very classic style of plant association, a uniformity of lower plants in front rising up to taller ones behind, plants in large blocks and, of course, the uniformity of using only herbaceous perennials and selected annuals. With no woody shrubs the overall texture is principally one of soft dome textures of flower and leaf punctuated by occasional verticals such as delphiniums. Many of the plants do not have individually strong form or architectural shapes, but massed together they grow up to perform in mid-summer, when the overall effect is one of unforgettable plant architecture.

Few people have the opportunity to garden on the scale of the borders at Arley, but the lesson they teach is universally applicable:

the essence of formal planting is that its neatness and symmetry should be in harmony with a certain freshness rather than induce a feeling of harshly imposed lines and shapes. Overdone, formality has a fussiness that stifles the easy sense of proportion that make it suitable to gardens of all sizes. Among all twentieth-century gardeners few have been so widely admired for their schemes of formal planting as Russell Page and he wrote instructively on the subject. For small gardens he considered that 'the principle of a small space near the house designed for flowers in a formal way adapts itself well to contemporary restrictions,' and went on to write more generally: 'I like to keep the pattern of a formal garden very simple and to use squares, circles and rectangles outlined by narrow paved paths and edge them, as often as not, with lavender, box, rosemary or santolina. I see them as gardens compartmented like a Persian rug, a series of simple shapes to fill with flowers in any one of a hundred different ways.'

Page's ideas continue a long-established traditon of formality in a garden, one that derives from an external structure, within which planting responds but is inevitably formal in appearance. As Roy Strong suggested right at the beginning of this chapter, and as we have seen in planting details of, for instance, Beth Chatto's garden, a quite different sense of formality can be introduced by relying purely on plant choice and association. Rather than having formality imposed by external, semi-architectural influences – hedges, adjoining paths or the straight-lined rectangular shape of a border – plants can create it themselves with their individual form and texture, or, by their repetition, giving a thread of continuity through a planting scheme.

Such an idea is closely in line with a philosophy of contemporary planting, that the plants and their characteristics dictate not only the individual colours and shapes, but also the overall dimensions and appearance of a planting. Where it has long been a goal to follow Rosemary Verey's idea of 'strong design softened by an exuberance of planting' – informality contained within formality – it is a new idea to be able to achieve formality through plant structure within a design of overall informality.

LEFT Formality on a majestic scale at Arley Hall. The architectural symmetry of the double herbaceous border leading to a central seat in a stone arbour is strengthened by the graduations of shape and colour in the detail of the plant groupings.

ABOVE Straight paths, clipped box, a classic stone urn: these traditional elements of a formal garden are brought to life by the exuberance of the summer roses, with their underplanting of hardy geraniums and other perennials.

PLANTING WITH WATER

'WATER IN THE GARDEN, WHETHER POND OR

STREAM, LAKESIDE OR ARTIFICIAL POOL, OFFERS

THE GARDENER TEMPTATIONS HARD TO RESIST.'

RUSSELL PAGE

Water has the ability to provide
planting with both a focus and the
priceless dimension of reflection; here
there is also a suggestion of harmony
between garden and countryside -
it could equally well be either.

That water is an enviable bonus for any gardener has been recognized for centuries. Its presence, in whatever form, adds a new dimension to a garden, and its potential relationship with plants offers delightful opportunities. Gertrude Jekyll, writing about water plants, reflected a shift of perception that began at the beginning of the twentieth century: as gardening became for many people a question of growing plants in different habitats, water assumed a role as yet another

Gardening a generation later, Russell Page approached the presence and use of water in a garden with the thoughtfulness that he lent to all his planting and design. He stressed the degree to which the presence of water is most rewarding when carefully integrated with planting and not used as the excuse for excessive celebration: 'Before your inner eye float luscious pictures of groups of iris and primula, willows and water-lilies and a mirage of picturesque details culled from books and exhibition catalogues.

LEFT The green and cream swords of *Iris pseudacorus* 'Variegata' combine beautifully with the 'Sweet Harmony' tulips planted on the drier bank above this waterside planting at the Manor House, Heslington.

RIGHT The formality of the canal at Abbotwsood immediately suggests a controlled style of associated planting, limited to groups of water lilies and clumps of iris.

plant habitat. In offering advice on streamside planting, she is firm on the matter of overgilding the lily: 'I should be careful not to crowd too many different plants into my stream-picture. Where the forget-me-nots are it would be quite enough to see them and the double Meadow-Sweet, and some good hardy moisture-loving Fern, Osmunda or Lady Fern. The way to enjoy these beautiful things is to see one picture at a time; not to confuse the mind with a crowded jumble of too many interesting individuals, such as is usually to be seen in a water-garden.'

Too much enthusiasm of this kind and you may quite likely damage your garden composition irretrievably.' Both Page and Jekyll recognized that if you are fortunate enough to have water in your garden it is not enough to purely embellish it with plants and hope for a perfect result. In some cases the initial framework for planting, the water itself, will benefit from alteration, in others, the balance in prominence between water and attendant plants needs to be varied.

Waterside plantings are most satisfying when they harmonize

in style with the water. The banks of a natural stream, for example, will often ask for very different plants and plant associations from a formal, square-edged pool prominently set in surrounding lawn. In the first case, any quantity, and especially any great variety, of planting might upset the pastoral atmosphere; in the second, the planting should not overplay its hand and smother either the architectural value of the pool surround or the mirror-like water surface. On the other hand, the very presence of water suggests lushness and the planting should not disappoint.

Beth Chatto's water garden, although man-made in an originally waterlogged area, is a naturalistic stream running between a series of ponds and her planting clothes the banks, drifts into the shallow water edges and extends away into moisture-retaining beds. In contrast, the main water feature at Tintinhull is a long rectangular pool in an axial position with the rest of the garden and with a loggia at one end. Its associated planting has an equally stately and restrained style. Yet despite these very different types of planting, each succeeds completely in being integrated into the

surrounding garden. Beth Chatto and Penelope Hobhouse both recognize that there are two fundamentally different and yet closely related elements that make for successful planting in and around water. In the first instance (as at Tintinhull), the association between planting and water is primarily visual, complementary, the plants an almost architectural focal point. In the second it is physical, the water itself providing the growing conditions for specific types of plants – the whole *raison d'être* for Beth Chatto's water garden.

What is perhaps most surprising, in a garden dominated by the region's harsh gardening conditions of paltry rainfall, high summer temperatures and soil that is mostly poor sand and gravel, is that Beth Chatto *has* a water garden. In fact, she has remarked, 'I doubt whether I would have made a water garden if I had not had a naturally wet site.' She may have needed an existing boggy patch to encourage her, but once she had begun Beth Chatto realized that much of the enjoyment lies in the variety of relationships between water and planting and the different conditions that can be created. Russell Page recognized the importance and potential in this variety of water 'moods', and suggested, for instance, consciously slowing the speed of running water to make the sense of movement more effective. This, he explained, could

LEFT The tapestry of plants that include yellow trollius and moisture-loving grasses instantly suggests the damp shady conditions that exist beneath this weeping willow.

RIGHT A rich variety of foliage shapes and textures is always possible with waterside planting. Here at the Manor House, Heslington, tall spikes contrast with lush flat circles offset by feathery fronds, into which the introduction of colour is a secondary ornament.

LEFT Bold single groupings of plants make up a picture reminiscent of a Monet painting: generous stands of *Iris laevigata* contrasting with luxuriant hostas leaves against a background of *Euphorbia griffithii* 'Fireglow'.

RIGHT Abundant plants arching from both banks over a narrow channel present one of the most invigorating of waterside plantings and is well demonstrated here by the mixtures of foliage intermingled with persicarias in Beth Chatto's canal garden.

be done either by subtle alterations to the watercourse itself or by the nature of planting on either side: 'Water which runs fast and uninterruptedly through and out of a garden may seem to drain away the garden's character. In such a case I like to widen it into a pool and give it time to pause. Carefully arranged planting too, can give the impression of steadying and slowing down the passage of a stream. Planting on both sides of a length of running water, however charming in detail, will only accentuate the sense of movement. Plant thickly with high plants and bushes in a wide bed designed as a single unit and placed at an angle to the flow; or let the stream run through a group of flowering or other trees planted on both banks, so that there is an alternation of light and shadow, level lawns and heavy planting.'

He could have been describing Beth Chatto's water garden. Its evolution has been governed by the same principles that are the

hallmark of her work throughout the garden. While the plants themselves are quite different in character and demand from those in other areas, they are all particularly well suited to their situation, and associations between them have been formed on the basis of shape and texture rather than flower colour. Two other influences that are consistent with the rest of the garden are the aim to build up semi-permanent plant colonies and the grouping of plants in flowing, informal lines that harmonize with, rather than impose upon, the natural (or in some areas the realigned) contours of the site.

The water garden itself was created by earth-moving on a large scale with a drag-line machine. Beth Chatto had in the back of her mind an important rule (reminiscent of Gertrude Jekyll's) that would apply to the subsequent planting. 'Plants suitable for water gardens range from those adapted to growing in the water itself,

such as water lilies and certain iris, through those found around the water's edge, marginal plants, like bog primulas, and finally to large perennials, like astilbes, ligularias and polygonums [persicarias], which need soil that is not waterlogged but remains damp throughout the summer. For a water garden to look natural this transition of soil conditions must already exist – or be provided.'

Put in such a way the establishment of plants in a water garden sounds deceptively simple. Beth Chatto's comment reveals how being firmly guided by such ground rules will assist plant combinations to assimilate into long-term harmony. Among the earliest plants added to the newly dug water garden were a selection of trees all suitable to the waterside and happy to stand in constantly damp ground: weeping willow (*Salix* × *sepulcralis chrysocoma*) and two beautiful dediduous evergreens, the swamp cypress (*Taxodium distichum*) and the dawn redwood (*Metasequoia glyptostroboides*) These three trees have grown up to frame the views which the creation of large areas of water opened up so dramatically.

Although the water garden's character and appearance evolved over a number of years, Beth Chatto always knew that the series of ponds and interlinking stream would provide the catalyst and centrepiece for planting that would extend away from the perimeters into the shade of trees and shrubs on both sides, presenting opportunities for enormously varied planting. At intervals along open pond edges strikingly different architectural shapes of foliage – luxuriant gunnera and lysichitons; sword-like grasses – alternate with sweeping plant colonies where the associations of foliage punctuated by a careful selection of flower colour perpetuate a constant feeling of plant luxuriousness. Powerful foliage shapes such as ligularias, hostas and rodgersias support more delicate-looking primulas, persicarias and astilbes. Moving away from sunny water's edge into more shady areas many of the plant effects, such as the newly unfolded fronds of ferns, are almost tactile. The sense of lushness, however, is not confused by an endless tapestry of different plants; rather, those that thrive in certain conditions are repeated where those conditions reappear – perhaps with different neighbours, but always in a manner guided

LEFT Candelabra primulas, bright yellow trollius and ranunculus punctuate groups of grasses to produce a plant landscape full of atmosphere in Beth Chatto's water garden, emphasizing a philosophy that pervades her whole garden.

RIGHT Green is the dominant colour of the palette when planting in or near water, its myriad different shades multiplied by an endless variety of shapes and textures.

by Beth Chatto's warning, 'It is important to assess the planting situation carefully. You simply cannot simply say this is the water-side, and so any damp-loving plant will grow here.'

Beth Chatto places few restrictions upon her choice of plants throughout the garden, but in the water garden it is important to site plants carefully and to avoid overdoing combinations. To this end, certain key plants – persicarias, ferns, trollius and hostas, for instance – reappear in a number of different places. In one water-side border the bright array of colour given by mixed candelabra primulas, blue irises and yellow ranunculus would be jarring without a softening, enveloping carpet of hostas and other foliage.

The water garden is given much of its impact by the size and texture of a selection of foliage plants that grow best either right in the shallow water's edge or in constantly damp soil close by. Both *Gunnera manicata* and *G. chilensis* demand such conditions to produce their vast crinkled umbrellas of foliage on tall prickled stems. (Both benefit from folding over the leaves to protect the crowns during winter.) The gunneras attain sufficient size to be

These luxuriant shapes provide bold statements against which the more angular iris leaves, grasses and sedges show up well. Running through the shallow water edges are spreading small-flowered aquatic native plants: *Caltha palustris*, the brilliant yellow-flowered marsh marigold, and *Myosotis scorpioides*, the water forget-me-not – both of which Gertrude Jekyll recommended growing. The tapestry of foliage shapes, textures and shades of green is extended by large round-leaved ligularias and some of the garden's many rodgersias.

From the water's edge the planting of the beds that flow through the water garden extends without perceptible break into soil that is constantly damp but without standing water, where the various astilbes and persicarias thrive, and to areas of deep shade beneath the trees, offering protection to the foliage of hostas and other sun-susceptible plants such as *Rodgersia podophylla* and one of the most elegant ferns, the ostrich plume fern (*Matteuccia struthiopteris*). As striking as the individual plants are, it is their combinations, layers of foliage overlapping around groups of plants that grow into vertical spires when in flower, that together make a constant succession of growth lasting from spring right through autumn. Early-flowering celandines and the hooded yellow arums are followed by the unfurling leaves of rodgersias and hostas, clumps of candelabra primulas in interwoven bright shades of white, pink, apricot and orange, and the wonderfully tight yellow buds of *Trollius europaeus*, the globe flower. Mauve, white and yellow irises are unfolding among their sword-like leaves and persicarias add their pink or mauve poker-shaped flowers to the vertical accents. Different astilbes flower through summer into autumn, while the ruddy shades of rodgersias are developing with the arched lines of grasses. Perhaps because it has an oasis quality compared to the other areas of the garden, in early summer this is a place of celebration that occasionally hints at turning to riot.

But the predominant palette is green, and one of the great qualities of the water garden is Beth Chatto's awareness that the flower colours – many shades of yellow for much of the year – are

able to shelter people during a sudden shower. The bog arums, *Lysichiton americanus*, whose yellow hooded flowers appear in spring and *L. camtschatensis*, with creamy flowers, make an equally bold statement when their shiny green shield-like leaves grow up after the flowers, as do the arum lilies, *Zantedeschia aethiopica*. Beth Chatto recommends the variety 'Crowborough', which survives happily outside if safely mulched during winter. These more stately waterside plants are usually most effective when grown individually and not mixed with other plants.

secondary to the background tapestry of foliage whose different shapes make great visual impact without the distraction of quantities of colour. Revelling in an atmosphere of damp warmth, many of the plants assume giant proportions or a luxuriant quality and here they are growing in an ideally expansive setting. The vast leaves of gunneras and rodgersias set the scale of the planting to match the setting, but whether with these imposing characters or the more delicate ferns and grasses, the shapes and textures of

At the temple and pool at Barnsley, the planting in early summer is contained to suit the scale and the element of formality in the situation.

foliage dominate the planting throughout the water garden. The growing conditions provided are such that plants will develop and maintain healthy foliage through more of the year than usual and the sense of naturalness that merging shades of green provide against water is something that should not be overrun by a misplaced enthusiasm for colour. Sufficient richness is readily available – as Beth Chatto's waterside confirms.

Beth Chatto's water garden is on a scale commensurate with the proportions that many of the waterside plants attain during summer and with the quantity of plants along the water's edge and filling the succession of beds. Although by no means separate from the other areas of the garden, it is, however, an independent, self-contained entity in its seasonal progression of growth and dying away to winter bareness. It is intriguing to see the contrast with the water features in Rosemary Verey's garden at Barnsley, created in a quite different situation, with different priorities, and yet with similar guidelines regarding the choice and combinations of plants.

The most formal element of the garden at Barnsley is the series of three parallel vistas that run side by side across the garden. The longest – and, according to Rosemary Verey, the most important – extends from the temple against one boundary wall to the fountain against the wall on the far side of the garden. At both ends water and accompanying planting are integral to the scene. As one looks from the main garden, a pool surrounded by old flagstones reflects the classical stone facade of the temple and provides the centrepiece of this area for sitting out. Its formal shape is ideally suited to the situation and complements the temple's architecture, but the formal lines are softened by planting both in the water and in the beds on three sides. These are kept permanently damp by water seeping from the pool through holes deliberately left during the construction.

Actually in the pool are water lilies, the most suitable aquatic plants for growing in a formal water setting. In the beds around marsh marigolds, *Caltha palustris*, are followed by blue-flowered *Iris sibirica*, the tall yellow *Primula florindae* and warm-hued hemerocallis (day lilies). The limitation of flower colour to yellow and blue ensures that the effect will not be busy in a way that would detract from the planting's role in the more general scheme of pool and temple vista. At the same time the choice of plants for this little pool garden ensures that the planting in this

relatively small-scale situation does not look contrived. The restricted area means that the marsh marigolds have to be controlled, unlike in Beth Chatto's water garden where they are free to spread at will.

The planting was always intended to be part of, but not dominate, the appearance and atmosphere of the pool garden. The limited range of flower colour, which is in evidence for some four months of the year, means that the foliage greens and shapes – the spikes of iris, the arching day lilies, the rounded plates of water

A number of plants here are similar to those in the previous picture, but at the Manor House, Heslington the atmosphere is immediately different; natural and informal, the scene illustrates the ability of water to merge garden and landscape and to make the same plants suitable to both.

lilies and luxuriant elephant's ears of bergenias – are the main feature for much of the time. Even with such a limited choice it is instructive that Rosemary Verey has achieved the cross-section of aquatic foliage, from the shiny exotic rounds of bergenias and water lilies to the strong, sharp verticals of the irises. The need to perpetuate the foliage throughout the year, to maintain its presence in the overall architectural scheme, is answered by a pair of *Phormium tenax*, the New Zealand flax, which flank the path as

Two views of the frog fountain at Barnsley. Viewed along the grass path from the temple and pool, it is a focal point that must integrate with the planting on either side. Close to, the fountain reveals its own delightful features and the planting in the immediate environment, although not necessarily of water-loving plants, has the lush appearance suitable to a watery setting.

it enters the pool garden and whose sword-like leaves make a strong statement all year round.

The surface of the pool is undisturbed so as not to obscure its reflections. But standing in front of the temple looking out across the garden the sound of water splashing in the frog fountain beckons you across the garden. This sense of movement, both of the water itself and through its powers of attraction, is a vital feature which was lacking until the fountain was introduced. The progression along the grass walk between pool and fountain subconsciously binds the areas of water and their planting with the rest of the garden.

The frog fountain is a design by the sculptor Simon Verity, in which four stone frogs spout water against a flat block of Purbeck stone, relief-carved with two sheep. The Purbeck stone is raised on a large block above the small fountain pool into which the water trickles and falls. Rosemary Verey explains how the introduction of water transformed this area. 'Suddenly the borders on either side of the fountain took on new importance. Before they were just at the end of the garden; now we and visitors were attracted there by the moving water. The spouting frogs gave a watery look to the area, and although the soil was no damper than in the nearby beds, plants had to be added to give an atmosphere of coolness and moisture … All the plants have large, important leaves and combine to transform this shady corner into a leafy scene.' Combining to produce the feeling of watery lushness without actually being aquatic, the predominant plants are angelica and various ligularias, with hostas and ferns behind the fountain and *Alchemilla mollis* frothing in front – but not high enough to obscure the water jets from view. Again, the primary emphasis is on foliage.

In the contemporary garden one of the most rewarding aspects of water is the wildlife it encourages and supports. The choice of plants around this haven is deliberately restrained and understated, limited to near-species that have been allowed to colonize the bank.

In Beth Chatto's garden, and in Rosemary Verey's on a smaller scale, the water is integral to the style and choice of plants used. It is a direct association from aquatics actually in the water to those in the surrounding soil that enjoy the constant damp. The same is true with Pam Lewis's even smaller, but completely natural, water garden at Sticky Wicket. She calls it the 'frog garden', and the name suggests the extent to which encouraging wildlife is important in this area, and as in many gardens the water and surrounding bogginess provides inrivalled opportunities for wildlife, whether frogs, toads and newts, or birds and an array of insects. In the area around the small pond the plants are restricted to those you might find growing in similar conditions in the wild: flag iris (*I. pseudacorus*) and marsh marigolds (*Caltha palustris*), with clumps of dogwoods, willow (*Cornus* and *Salix* spp.) and rubus on the far side from the house providing a screen of coloured stems

in winter. Pam Lewis's frog garden demonstrates how water planted in a natural style can be restricted to a very small scale – even if it does require occasional management to accommodate the wildife and the planting: 'Paddling in the squelchy pond in December to clear excess vegetation is worth the discomfort and chill to watch frogs spawning in March.'

From water at its most informal to water as an architectural feature: the pool garden at Tintinhull. The pool is in reality a long rectangular canal, set in symmetrically shaped rectangular lawns on either side and bounded by borders and yew hedges. There is a classical pillared loggia or summerhouse at one end and a vista through the 'doorway' in the hedges opposite. It is a fundamentally classical, formal scene, taking its cue from the water, and the associated planting has to harmonize with this.

The spatial quality of the expanse of water set in neat lawn and reflecting its surroundings, what Penelope Hobhouse calls 'the volume of space' would be diminished by quantities of planting close to the water's edge and, anyway, the architectural treatment, the paved stone surround, suggests that this would be inappropriate. At the same time it is important to appreciate how the paths through the different adjacent garden compartments at Tintinhull all gravitate towards arriving at the view across the pool to the summerhouse: it is, says Penelope Hobhouse, 'the natural centre of the whole garden'. Given the intimate character of many of the other compartments and the emphasis on planting in most of them, this is a chance for the contrast of an architectual flourish whose impact is all the more for being a surprise discovery.

And so the lines of the central composition are enhanced with planting, but with reticence. In the water, confined to the four

The other image of water in the garden: formal and architectural. Here at Tintinhull the pool garden is the focus of paths and vistas from adjacent enclosures, and in such a situation the planting echoes and enhances both the garden's visual style and its mood, with the careful arrangement of water lilies, irises and planted pots to suit the setting.

corners of the pool, are reflecting clumps of yellow-flowered *Iris pseudacorus*. In mid-summer red and white water lilies produce their tablecloths of shiny leaves in carefully controlled patches against the stone edges. They enhance, but are never allowed to upstage, the water's reflective quality and its basic unadorned symmetry; this is undisturbed. Instead, set sufficiently far back across the lawn on either side, the two borders down the long sides, both backed by yew hedges, complete the pool garden's character. Their richness of planting, described in detail in Chapter 2, is sufficiently removed from the pool to act as a positive enhancement of its architectural symmetry. Positioned any closer they would crowd it unacceptably; where they are, especially on a summer's day, they proffer a wealth of colourful planting that – by dint of being an opposite – increases the sense of well-ordered coolness of the water itself.

The pool garden's formality and axial position within the garden as a whole neatly illustrates the effectiveness with which water can provide a garden's major focal point. A pool can provide the keynote to a garden's design, the unifying feature around which the rest of the garden pulls together. At the same time it can be a visual focus, the water's reflective quality emphasizing this if given a sufficiently spacious setting.

The appearance and atmosphere of Tintinhull's pool garden is comparable (on a different scale) to the pool in front of the temple at Barnsley, but quite different from Beth Chatto's or Pam Lewis's water gardens. None the less, the association of water and planting in all four follows many similar guidelines. The balance between the two elements, water and plant life, should always be respected and, as we have seen different situations, may demand a different emphasis in the relationship. Where the water has an architectural role, the associated planting should respect this and probably be confined to few varieties used in repetition. Where the water provides the basic habitat, as at Sticky Wicket and in Beth Chatto's garden, the atmosphere of lushness should not be confused by over-enthusiastic random planting that has no sense of associations or combinations.

THE KITCHEN GARDEN

'IF I TELL YOU YOU SHOULD MAKE UP YOUR MIND AT

THE OUTSET WHETHER THE VEGETABLE IN QUESTION

IS FOR CARNAL OR FOR SPIRITUAL DEGUSTATION, YOU

MAY FAIRLY REPLY YOU FULLY INTEND TO HAVE THE

BEST OF BOTH WORLDS, AND TO GROW YOUR GLOBE

ARTICHOKES IN THE FLOWER BORDER.'

CHRISTOPHER LLOYD

The low hedges of clipped box, *Buxus
sempervirens* 'Latifolia Maculata', that
enclose the potager beds give both a
formal edging and here add textural
contrast to the purple foliage of
young ornamental cabbages.

Christopher Lloyd's comment suggests a dilemma about where you should grow vegetables. What it reflects, however, is the acceptance among contemporary gardeners that the kitchen garden is not an inferior place to 'ornamental' gardens. In fact, it can be highly attractive and achieves this to best effect when fruit and vegetables are grown together with flowers. This does not necessarily mean mixing them up together, although many gardeners now do. Rather, it means creating a composition where blocks or rows of vegetables are perhaps divided or edged with flowering perennials and grown next to a border of wall shrubs which might be alternating with fruit trees trained against a boundary wall.

Gertrude Jekyll wrote: 'I have often thought what a beautiful bit of summer gardening one could do, mainly with things usually grown in the kitchen garden only and filling up spaces with quickly-growing plants.' Today her advice can be followed in most planting situations, especially in spring and early summer when, as she suggests, there are spaces to be filled. Perennial, annual or biennial herbs are ideal for inclusion among herbaceous plants: angelica for its statuesque foliage, or fennel for height; borage or

LEFT In the arched tunnel in Rosemary Verey's potager the flowering plants – sunflowers, pot marigolds and nasturtiums – all have kitchen garden associations. Frilly lettuces such as 'Lollo Rosso' further contribute to the potager's ornamental character.

RIGHT Deep red ruby chard planted with sedums demonstrate how vegetables can be mixed adventurously with other garden plants.

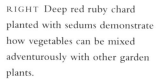

The arrangement of Barnsley's potager shows how the pattern of plants is designed to complement and strengthen the geometric framework. And yet within the orderly arrangement the sense of a constant cycle as different plants grow up and are then replaced by others removes the danger of the rigidity of an unchanging scene.

hyssop for misty blue flowers and chives for a neat front edging – only the more rampant ones such as tarragon and mint become too invasive to be let loose in the border. Many vegetables have outstanding ornamental foliage to set off other plants: the deeply serrated, arching leaves of cardoons and the closely related globe artichokes; the blood-red stems of chard with a tracery of vein-like patterns in the shiny purple-green leaves; all kinds of lettuce and cabbage, green and purple, crinkly or tight-bunched; as well as various runner beans with their different coloured flowers for training up canes or netting. The trailing stems of larger-leaved squashes can be trained in the same way. All of these are equally suited to being integrating into a border as for growing among the orderly ranks of a traditional kitchen garden.

Gertrude Jekyll's idea of 'decorating' the vegetable area with flowering plants is not new, but can be traced back to the potager,

which originated in France. Here, the aim was to arrange vegetables and associated plants in a formalized pattern, the most famous being the enormous potager of the sixteenth-century château of Villandry. Nobody today creates a potager on the scale of Villandry, but the attraction of the intricacy of paths, clipped hedges, structural features and vegetables arranged to make a pattern survives. It also provides an important element in modern gardens: the priority of continuity, of utilizing the garden as a year-round feature rather than planting for seasonal highlights.

It is in the kitchen garden, rather than in the integration of ornamental vegetables into a border, that the most exciting potential of kitchen garden planting lies. The kitchen gardens that supplied great Edwardian country houses often had impressive double herbaceous borders stretching along either side of their central paths and all manner of fruit trees trained against the walls.

A combination of neat productivity and some decorative planting make up an archetypal kitchen garden.

But, the kitchen garden was kept quite separate from the ornamental gardens, and often no one other than the gardening staff ever went there. Today the kitchen garden, if treated as a mixed garden, can happily be the most important – or even the only – area of garden, as Penelope Hobhouse observed about the kitchen garden she extensively replanned at Tintinhull: 'the Tintinhull kitchen garden is attractive enough on its own to provide a model for the main area of any modest-sized house.'

In some ways the incentive for planting fruit, vegetables and flowers in a style that rises above the utilitarian background of growing for the kitchen comes from the idea not to 'pigeonhole' plants that Christopher Lloyd advocated in Chapter 1. But this is

not the only impetus. Rarely has the growing of fruit and vegetables for both productive and ornamental purposes been more enthusiastically pursued in gardens of all sizes. This is influenced by our attitudes to what we eat, our concern about where it has come from and how free of chemicals its cultivation has been. Second, edible and ornamental, as Christopher Lloyd suggests, gives exciting potential. In the smallest town garden it is quite likely that a number of containers or one of the limited areas of cultivation will be given over to herbs and a selection of favourite salad plants. In large gardens open to the public, increasingly the area of greatest fascination for visitors is a full-scale working kitchen garden complete with glasshouses, fruit cages and forcing pits.

During the 1960s and 1970s owners of country houses with traditional walled kitchen gardens ripped out plants and greenhouses and put in tennis courts and swimming pools. Not today. While we are unikely to see the return of glasshouses devoted to the cultivation of Malmaison carnations as were common in Edwardian days, and while large areas will possibly be left as grass, it is definitely in the kitchen garden where the gardening goal is a balance of visual interest and productivity.

This careful balance of vegetables, fruit and flowers – including shrubs, perennials and bulbs – is exemplified in the kitchen garden at Tintinhull. The key to the success is the style in which the kitchen garden theme is retained by the 'productive' plants, but expanded and enhanced by the addition of borders around the vegetables and by rows of seasonal flowers that are raised in the kitchen garden for planting out later elsewhere. 'Many of the new plants have a semi-domestic connotation or are useful herbs,' says Penelope Hobhouse, 'which makes them especialy suitable for growing adjacent to vegetables. There are shrub roses with apple-like hips, gilded rosemary ... southernwood, lavenders, lovage, *Salvia officinalis*, angelicas (both the stately *Angelica archangelica* for preserving and the less common *A. gigas*, with bronze stems, from Asia).' Two examples of plants among the vegetables that combine productivity and decoration are forget-me-nots grown from seed sown in rows in the kitchen garden in June from which the young plants are later transplanted to their chosen place, and rows of dahlia tubers whose late-summer flowers will enliven the neighbouring vegetables.

Golden marjoram with the powder-blue foliage of young brassicas (left) and bright helichrysums among more mature Brussels sprouts demonstrate how herbs and everlasting flowers for cutting can bring a zing of colour to rows of vegetables.

Sited in one corner of the grounds, the kitchen garden at Tintinhull is bordered on two sides by old boundary hedging, with new hedges planted by Penelope Hobhouse to enclose the perimeter on the third and fourth sides. Openings through these new hedges provide vistas to adjacent areas, encouraging a link and planting harmony with the rest of the garden. Within, the garden's traditional layout consists of four rectangular quarters enclosed by an outer path on all sides and divided by cross-paths at right angles.

A large-scale vegetable garden demands certain practicalities in its layout and cultivation, including constant easy access to growing areas, the ability to plant out in rows, and the need for adjacent areas to be at different stages of preparation for different seasonal crops. Unadorned, the effect can be stark and rigid; by adding borders along the paths, each of different character and planting style, and with plants actually among the rows of produce, the garden's season is extended right through the year, with ornamental plants from late-winter bulbs onwards enlivening the annual cycle of vegetables. As Penelope Hobhouse explains, 'Although the centre beds are used primarily for vegetables we also treat them as a nursery for the whole garden, sowing the seed of annuals and biennials in rows among the lettuce, beans and cabbage.' In addition, rows of sweet peas trained over a bamboo frame and dahlias alternated with the vegetables both provide cut flowers for the house.

The main path through the centre of the garden is lined first by massed narcissi and later by a carpet of the large catmint, *Nepeta* 'Six Hills Giant'. At right angles the shorter path has spring planting of tulips, narcissi, forget-me-nots and primroses to be followed by prolific pink-flowered shrub roses in front of espalier pears. As the roses are coming to an end, bushes of *Caryopteris × clandonensis* 'Heavenly Blue' between them contribute their clear blue puffballs through into autumn. These permanent, regular plantings are merged with one of the kitchen garden's best features – self-seeding perennials whose sometimes random appearance softens the overall geometry of the rows. Here, they are the spiky-branched and flat-flowered purple *Verbena bonariensis* and mauve-flowered musk mallow. In other surrounding borders – and sometimes encroaching beyond – brunneras and fritillaries, aquilegias, symphytum, sweet rocket (*Hesperis matronalis*), martagon lilies and poppies are just some of the plants that spread happily between the more permanent groups of shrubs and perennials.

These borders around the vegetable beds were originally used for individual plants that would later be put out in other parts of the garden. The best were left to establish themselves and have grown to structural proportions, and have had others added around them, so that on all sides the planting has developed way beyond the original intent. The result is a series of strong plant statements around the kitchen garden: a pair of ornamental pear trees framing the view into the adjacent fountain garden; the arching perennial grass *Stipa gigantea* similarly punctuating the corners below steps from the pool garden; great blocks of *Euphorbia characias wulfenii* 'John Tomlinson' around which groups of cistus, asters and treasures such as *Gaura lindheimeri*, have grown up. Along one edge, in front of a boundary holly hedge, pink-flowered 'Wolley-Dod' roses tower behind old-fashioned crinums that will flower in late summer; along another a yew hedge is fronted with red apothecary's roses (*Rosa gallica officinalis*) facing a long raised bed at its best in spring. The succession of planting provides constant change as you progress round the garden, framing both the regimented vistas along paths, and the more varied glimpses through into the central areas.

Tintinhull illustrates the multi-faceted character that a kitchen garden can achieve: full of its own interest and visual charm but also connected with other areas of a larger garden by being the productive nursery for borders and beds elsewhere. Perhaps the only traditional feature the Tintinhull kitchen garden lacks is old walls for training fruit trees, wall plants and climbers. Otherwise the integration of vegetables, fruit and flowers has been established to a degree where it is – as Penelope Hobhouse acknowledges – a mixed garden rather than just a kitchen garden. In many ways this looks back to the traditonal role of the Victorian and Edwardian kitchen gardens, but the adventurous mixture of planting around and among the fruit and vegetables is perhaps the most contemporary element. One of the lessons to be learnt from Tintinhull – and which when successfully achieved is a primary appeal of kitchen gardening in general – is the manner in which the decorative nature of planting is still desirable, but balanced by a need for productivity and a strong sense of seasonal progression. Even in the depths of winter, when there may only be a few shrub shapes and seedheads in the main borders, there are winter vegetables for cutting and, quite possibly, some tiny early bulbs emerging in one hidden-away area.

The rectangular kitchen garden at Tintinhull measures nearly 60×30 m (some 200×100 ft). By the standards of most gardens it is a large area, which partly accounts for the rich diversity that Penelope Hobhouse achieved. But it is only about half the size of the recently restored areas of walled kitchen garden at West Dean House in Sussex. It is particularly interesting to see how the restoration at West Dean has succeeded in evoking the garden's Edwardian heyday – for instance, concentrating on varieties of plants known to have been used in the early twentieth century – while at the same time presenting an immaculate composition

In this view across the kitchen garden of West Dean there is a satisfying sense of richness and symmetry in the spreading leaves of brassicas, parsley, rhubarb and globe artichokes.

LEFT Espaliered fruit trees, such as this yet-to-ripen 'Orleans Reinette' apple, were an important feature of traditional decorative kitchen gardens and remain equally rewarding today.

RIGHT In the main kitchen garden area of West Dean the central flower borders lead to a bench at one end. The ornamental planting, with an emphasis on hot colours, includes *Heuchera micrantha diversifolia* 'Palace Purple', rudbeckias, anthemis, calendulas and hemerocallis. In the background sunflowers grow up in front of fruit trees trained on the brick wall.

FAR RIGHT Traditional kitchen garden practices and implements are a feature of West Dean, typified by this group of sea kale with old-fashioned forcing pots to cover the young plants.

that enables visitors to appreciate the scope of kitchen gardening today. From 1992 to 1995 the head gardener, Jim Buckland, with his wife Sarah, oversaw the garden's restoration for West Dean's owners, the Edward James Foundation. They have subsequently organized its steady development and annual cultivation, with education for the garden's many visitors as much of a priority as the visual appearance.

As was the pattern in the Edwardian garden, the central area of restored glasshouses and the frame yard divide the upper ground, which is the main vegetable garden, and the lower ground, devoted to fruit trees. The vegetable garden, with a gently sloping south-facing aspect, is divided into traditional quarters. One of the central paths is flanked by borders planted with perennials and annuals to produce hot late-summer reds, oranges and yellows. Espalier fruit trees back these borders, making a boundary between them and the rows of vegetables that fill the main areas.

The central crossing in the other direction leads beneath a series of metal arches with pear trees trained over. The garden is an education in both how to grow vegetables and in the huge range of different varieties: West Dean grows about a hundred different kinds of vegetables – some are rare, but others easily available from seed suppliers.

There is a similar rich variety in the fruit trees of the lower ground. Again, it is divided into four areas by right-angled paths lined by borders – in one direction herbaceous plants with flowers of yellow, white and blue; in the other pink and pastel roses. As would have been the case in the original garden, the borders are designed to be in flower between the blossom and fruit seasons of the apple trees which are planted in grass in the four sections. Peaches, nectarines and apricots, which require maximum sun for ripening, are trained against the south-facing wall, with pears, plums and morello cherries against the north-facing

for its inspiration, but despite the scale it demonstrates many principles that apply to any size of plot. The garden presents itself in such a manner as to emphasize that it is the organization of kitchen gardening – the annual rotations, the choosing of suitable fruit and vegetable neighbours, the use of perennial flower borders for permanent planting – that is the key to success. Many

traditional crafts are taught and nurtured at West Dean, and one of the garden's great fascinations is the way in which the background to and practicalities of the planting and management are explained to visitors, with the result that these often appear far simpler than previously imagined.

The quantity and variety of plants in the various borders at both Tintinhull and West Dean have grown up to make two kitchen gardens where the fruit and vegetables are part of a broad spectrum – a garden complete from one season to the next. They make a fascinating comparison with Rosemary Verey's potager at Barnsley, smaller in scale and quite different in design. Here, the manner of gardening is intensive (the garden area is far smaller than at Tintinhull) and, because of its underlying formality, more exaggerated than in a traditional kitchen garden. The layout of a potager must begin with an initial structure of paths dividing patterned beds. Rosemary Verey explains: 'I made the basic design of

one. The garden has not been restored with a view to being ornamental, rather to demonstate the productivity of a large-scale kitchen garden. And yet the combination of immaculately worked and composted earth, the orderly rows, the adjacent textures of different top-growth and the atmosphere of burgeoning vitality through many months of the year makes for a garden of exhilarating display.

West Dean may be a country house kitchen garden of unusual size and intensity of planting that looks back to an illustrious past

the paths and beds many years ago, and this, with the framework of trees and shrubs, is permanent. Within the beds, though, the planting changes from year, but every season we try to have different patterns and colour effects.' This is achieved by a well-organized rotation of crops and plants combined: early salads and summer vegetables, for instance, beginning to emerge to accompany daffodils, tulips and apple blossom in spring. The paths, made either of old brick or paving, are lined mainly with clipped box hedging, but also with lavender and alpine strawberries, to give continual symmetry to the beds. Not only do these border plants give structure but, as Penelope Hobhouse suggested, they are entirely suitable kitchen garden plants. The structural pattern is accentuated by clipped box balls and pyramids at the corners of the beds. Apple and pear trees trained into different shapes add a vertical quality to the permanent planting, as well as providing spring blossom and autumn fruits, while 'White Pet' standard roses around the potager's central apple tree are also intrinsic to the pattern.

Within the overall design it is, however, the changing patterns of vegetables that are most representative of the potager and which require constant planning. 'The beds have their regular rotation of crops,' explains Rosemary Verey, 'always including salad, roots, brassicas, beans and peas … The two quarters beyond the central feature each have four small squares, perfect for growing climbing peas in diagonal rows. One bed has a permanent planting of artichokes, and the others are used for quick-maturing lettuce interplanted with cabbages or cauliflowers. The leeks are always interplanted with red lettuce or chicory and when the

and flowering peas twine upwards together, tall hollyhocks (*Alcea rosea*) and self-seeding Welsh poppies (*Meconopsis cambrica*) soften the lines of box-hedged paths and a medley of clambering peas, nasturtiums and gourds cover an arched metal tunnel above yellow-flowered *Rudbeckia* 'Marmalade'.

Rosemary Verey's potager was inspired by the seventeenth-

LEFT This scarecrow guarding crops of gooseberries has great traditional appeal. Adding to the charm of the scene are a flowering 'Iceberg' rose and honeysuckle in the background.

RIGHT Rows of pale yellow tulips and newly emerging salad and vegetable crops give a sense of orderliness in late spring that is retained by the potager's symmetrical design as the crops develop to maturity though the weeks of summer.

peas mature the ground is quickly filled by broccoli. Onions and lettuce are good companions and the root vegetables, carrots, parsnips and spinach, are sometimes sown in artistic triangles and sometimes in straight rows, as the mood of the moment dictates.'

Such well-planned rotation ensures that the patterns and colour displays are kept up. Salad crops, with their variety of foliage colours and shapes and requiring a shorter time to mature than other vegetables, are the constant staple. The patterns of vegetables are also enlivened with flowers at different seasons. In the spring, tulips and narcissi flower with the fruit blossom, and through the summer sweet peas, nasturtiums (*Tropaeolum majus*)

century gardening books of William Lawson, but its concept of presenting vegetables decoratively within a structure of other plants is entirely in sync with contemporary style. Small gardens often do not have room for vegetables in rows, nor are they large enough for the kitchen garden – bare for much of the year if unassisted by other planting – to be hidden away. At the same time, many people want to grow a limited variety of vegetables – as Penelope Hobhouse wants from her new garden 'only my favourites' – and not the quantities that can end up filling both every available gardening hour and every corner of larder, fridge and deep freeze. At Bourton House, in Gloucestershire, the kitchen garden is a tiny potager, tucked away in a sunken enclosure on the site of an old conservatory, but the same spirit is evident: there are espalier apples on the walls, beds are edged in green and variegated miniature box, and there is a predominance of salads arranged in patterns of green and purple, curly and domed, with some other limited introductions, such as carrots with beetroot and herbs.

The urge to grow fruit, herbs and vegetables in a patterned style, whether so detailed as Rosemary Verey's at Barnsley, or just a simple arrangement of four squares divided by brick paths around a central pyramid of, say, clipped box, has practical as well as artistic origins. Not surprisingly, Roy Strong, whose taste favours formality, has good advice. 'Like a herb garden, a potager demands a firm yet practical groundplan with elements of year-round interest to compensate for the empty beds in winter and the harvesting of crops in summer. Like the herb garden too, the potager needs shelter to protect the vegetables and establish a micro-climate in order to prolong the growing season. This calls for walls, hedges or some form of fencing which can take espaliered fruit trees. Within, you should divide it with paths and place a focal point, such as a pyramid of bay, a sundial, a terracotta pot, or even a dwarf fruit tree trained as a dome or a goblet, at the centre … Make a symmetrical pattern of paths, each wide enough to take a wheelbarrow and give easy access for working. You may then build on that geometry in the growing months by the way you plant your vegetables. Spinach, beet, cauliflowers, parsnips, potatoes, onions, French beans and cabbages all look different, so give a thought to their placing apart from the usual considerations of pure practicality, so that there is always a pleasant contrast of shape and colour.'

The potager offers a way to grow vegetables that is decorative and suited to a small area, making a combination of productivity and ornament that is one of the appeals of kitchen garden planting. It can be quite self-sufficient, your only garden. The potager is different from the kitchen garden, which may be decorative in its own right but serves primarily as supplier to the rest of the

LEFT A tunnel of metal arches makes a strong link between the main potager at Barnsley and the area beyond, screened by apples. From both ends the view beneath the arches is a continuous medley through the summer of tall sunflowers, nasturtiums clambering up the frames and a mixture of other flowering plants that usually includes the brilliant orange of marigolds and rudbeckias.

RIGHT Another example of a tunnel vista being imaginatively decorated with plants suitable to the kitchen garden; here a mixture of gourds in shades of yellow and green whose twining stems and foliage provide a thick canopy for months.

garden and to the kitchen. Here, a row of peas will grow next to pricked-out seedlings of hardy annuals waiting to go into a border, a block of potatoes leads to one of chrysanthemums for cutting or, even more evocative, furry-flowered sweet williams, *Dianthus barbatus*.

Perhaps more than most other areas of planting, the development of a kitchen garden produces greater similarity in the approach of different gardeners. As all the gardens in this chapter have shown, the element of creating a mood as well as a planting picture results in people having a similar approach even if the area and scale, or the design framework, are dramatically different. The idea that arranging certain vegetables together as companions to make the most of their variations in foliage; the importance of fruit trees to remain faithful to the 'complete' kitchen garden idea; the use of kitchen garden ground (where space allows) to grow on plants destined for borders elsewhere; all these run through the contemporary attitude. Decorating a kitchen garden so as to enliven but not overshadow the seasonal cycle of productivity should combine with the enjoyment of growing to eat; as George Eliot wrote over a century ago: 'No finical separation between flower and kitchen garden there; no monotony of enjoyment for one sense to the exclusion of another; but a charming paradisiacal mingling of all that was pleasant to the eyes and good for food.'

PLANTING CONTAINERS

'CONTAINER PLANTING SHOULD BE A COMBINATION OF SEVERAL DISCIPLINES, THOSE OF THE ARTIST, FLOWER ARRANGER, GARDENER AND PLANTSMAN.'

PAUL WILLIAMS

Beth Chatto extends her enjoyment of plant colonies to her containers. Rather than one tub or pot she arranges groups to present a vibrant and yet harmonized scene, a balance of shape and colour. Her choice of plants, *Helichrysum petiolare* and pelargoniums for instance, focuses on a number of widely used container favourites, while the swords of *Agave americana* 'Marginata' add a note of boldness and permanence to the composition.

Pots and tubs, and the plants they contain, have become an integral part of any good gardener's repertoire. Paul Williams, who has the Cotswold garden of Bourton House in his care, sees them drawing together the different skills that produce good planting in the larger garden, but focusing them more intensely. Artistry is needed, he suggests, in the association of colours, a flower-arranger's skill in composing with different shapes and textures, gardening ability crucial for healthy plants and plantsmanship to enable you to be confidently adventurous in your choice. This may sound daunting, but if your containers are under the spotlight, they also provide, says Paul Williams, 'one of the most rewarding styles of gardening; the ephemeral nature of the plantings allows plenty of scope for experimentation. Mistakes can be put right the next season and some new idea tried.' For, while container gardening is inextricably reliant on the skills that guide you in the garden at large, there is a subtle difference: when siting and planting a container it is almost as though you are creating a theatrical stage and the level of attention that a planted container can expect, compared to the rest of your garden, is undoubtedly higher. 'Containers', says Carol Skinner of Eastgrove Cottage reassuringly, 'are tremendous fun.'

They are fun for a number of reasons. Mobile, instant and changeable through the seasons (as is demonstrated with great bravado by Christopher Lloyd at Great Dixter), they can either extend and complement long-term planting style and appearance in a border, or make a direct contrast. They are, in a sense, a garden in microcosm, offering versatility of a sort no other planting situation approaches. They are the chance for sleight of hand or tricks; the interplay of architectural and planting shapes; a static element to contrast with the movement and rhythm of plants in and around them. They can embellish a garden scheme with a flourish or make a far gentler addition; part of the seasonal round and yet not controlled by it.

Containers can give a more comfortable feel to an area for sitting, and also enable planting to be brought right to the door on a paved terrace where it would be otherwise impossible. Not least

because they are often sited next to or close to the house, where you see and pass them constantly, they offer the chance for constant pampering to ensure a visual quality that is often not practical in the larger, permanent planting of your garden. 'Most important are the tubs by my study door, which I go through ten or twenty times a day,' says Rosemary Verey, 'the nearer you are to your 'home base' the more interesting the planting should be.' This focus of attention can take on many different guises. It can be intensely horticultural so that, for instance, such containers are planted with temperamental rarities that demand regular care and

LEFT The impact of this planting is intensified by being a container colony. This helps guarantee the kind of unified climax presented by the mixed argyranthemums, verbena, ivy-leafed pelargonium and hebes.

ABOVE In one large pot at Barnsley the silver and white of helichrysums and argyranthemums are dotted with the blue of *Felicia amelloides* and offset by the strong-shaded *Berberis thunbergii* 'Rose Glow' in the background.

LEFT This disparate collection of pots is lent unity by the pink and mauve colour scheme of the plants. Argyranthemums, pelargoniums and heliotropes all enjoy the sheltered site in the lee of the dry-stone wall, and their flower colours are linked to nearby planting by the deep purple clematis hugging the wall behind.

RIGHT For Pam Lewis it is important that her containers blend in with their immediate surroundings, so this *Dianthus alpinus* is complemented by the *Geranium sanguineum striatum* next to it. The terracotta dish emphasizes the low mat form of the dianthus more than simply planting it in the border, and also demonstrates how effective it is to use plants perhaps not immediately thought of as candidates for container planting.

attention. Or they can create an instant mood, which is what Rosemary Verey is looking for just outside her study door: 'With these tubs close to my doorway I have a feeling of summer exuberance immediately I walk out into the garden.'

The very choice of container for different plants is important. Rosemary Verey's courtyard tubs are old wooden half-barrels, their metal rings rusty with age. Russell Page liked only plain pots, preferably terracotta, for flowers. Too much decoration in the form of swags or other embellishments can distract the eye from the planting and should be used instead as ornament in its own right. White-painted wooden tubs, such as the classic square *caisses de Versailles*, are ideal for permanent evergreens such as lemon trees and clipped box standards but are usually too formal and architectural to offer the soft background that best offsets multi-coloured planting. Big pots make superb statements – as in the pool garden at Tintinhull – but can crowd the available space in a small garden. On the other hand, small ones often look lost on their own and should be clustered together to make their own miniature garden as Beth Chatto does, perhaps with some raised on blocks or to make tiers, thereby adding a vertical dimension to the composition.

Many successful planting schemes, especially those using shrubs or a combination of perennials, need several seasons to grow together into maturity and so take time to achieve the effect you are looking for. A well-planted pot, by contrast, can bring instant transformation and then last for weeks. Two points are advocated by our leading gardeners. First, there are few plants not suitable for growing in a pot or tub (and it is essential to look beyond the group of traditionally accepted candidates). Second, a container frothing with a mêlée of half a dozen summer annuals can be picturesque and lively, but often a combination limited to two or three different plants proves more effective and easier to enjoy.

The regularly made point that container planting should be guided by similar principles that apply to the rest of the garden is well illustrated by the need for harmony of flowers and foliage. It is a point made by Gertrude Jekyll and subsequently echoed and

similarly illustrated by others. She describes the suitable area of her garden where she concentrated her pots, before going on to outline the guiding principles. 'I have such a space in a cool court nearly square in shape. A middle circle is paved and all next to the house is paved, on a level of one shallow step higher. It is on the sides of this raised step that the pot plants are grouped, leaving free access to a wooden seat in the middle, and a clear way to a door on the

left. The first thing is to secure good greenery. On each side three oblong Italian terra-cotta pots full of Funkia [Hosta] grandiflora stand on the lower level. They serve to hide the common flower pots that are ranged behind ...' Having described the flowering plants that she uses, predominantly lilies, as well as irises, gladioli and Canterbury bells (*Campanula medium*), she adds: 'There are seldom more than two kinds of flowering plants placed here at a time; the two or three sorts of beautiful foliage are in themselves delightful to the eye; often there is nothing with them but Lilies, and one hardly desires to have more. There is an ample filling of the green plants, so no pots are seen.'

LEFT The lushness of *Hosta sieboldiana* is exaggerated to the point of being theatrical when allowed to realize its full size in a suitably architectural stone pot.

RIGHT A Beth Chatto pot colony is given a rich and exotic apppearance by the brilliant *Cyrtanthus elatus* in the foreground.

Beth Chatto concentrates the pots in her garden in two areas, both – Gertrude Jekyll would approve – adjacent to the house. One is a terrace at the foot of a flight of steps, the other the little courtyard outside her office. In both areas the desired effect is achieved by clustering pots together, the planting sufficient to overcome the ordinary appearance of their containers. 'By the end of summer,' she explains, 'the containers (whether handsome terracotta pots or plain black plastic buckets) become hidden in the enveloping trails of foliage and flower.' Exotic, architectural succulents such as aeonicum and cotyledon, with cordylines and agaves, are planted singly in pots to give strong foliage structure to sprays of ivy-leaved geraniums and helichrysum spreading out of others. Her aim in this sort of combination is that of a small-scale garden to be imported into an area previously devoid of planting, with a flexibility of shapes that one or two larger pots would not be able to offer. The mixture of plants – most of which would not grow happily or suitably elsewhere in the garden – also continues her overriding ideas about plant associations that combine foliage and flowers and a strong element of seasonal continuity.

Beth Chatto's pot garden is one small area of a larger whole. For many people such an area is their whole garden. Such close interrelation creates a permanent bond with the house, with the planting suggesting the constant interplay of rooms and garden space. Beth Chatto's office yard is a room, albeit an outdoor one, as definitely as the courtyard outside Rosemary Verey's study. But the liveliness and flexibility of planted containers for linking indoors and outdoors is never better demonstrated than at Great Dixter. As you approach the house from a gateway in a yew hedge, down the straight path with trees and meadow grass on either sides, the clusters of planted pots around the timber and tiled porch of the house beckon you all the way, greeting as well as offering a marriage of house and garden that constantly changes through the seasons.

In spring there are many choice narcissi, different varieties planted singly to a pot. There will also be tulips and wallflowers, again massed in single varieties. Through the summer the jostling array changes constantly, with a mixture of lilies, half-hardy or tender perennials and annuals and colourful exotics such as tall cannas. At all times different plants join the display when approaching their best and are replaced before their time is over, ensuring a constant sheen of freshness. As with Beth Chatto's garden, the choice of container is secondary to the plants them-selves. Many of the plants are those also grow in the open garden, but the cluster of pots in the porch gives an opportunity for con-stant experimentation with colours and shapes next to each other. An adventurous gardener such as Christopher Lloyd will constantly be looking at new associations and plant neighbours; some get on famously, other do not but can be changed in an

instant. In such a prominent position the change-overs take place far more often than is practical – or desirable – in the garden's borders, and have the effect of announcing to visitors the garden's changing mood on a far more regular basis than the more general seasonal changes from spring to summer, autumn and winter.

Containers are often structural as well as decorative, and their positioning needs planning. Russell Page, whose style of garden design often involved simple, elegant formal schemes enhanced by planted containers, once remarked that, 'pots should always, so to speak, have their feet firmly on the ground'. Rather than just being thoughtlessly plonked into position they should have an obvious role in any given place. In a formal scheme they must emphasize and be part of the design, on the corners of a square or at the junction of paths.

Penelope Hobhouse demonstrated this with great effect in the formal pool garden at Tintinhull. The long rectangular pool is the architectural centrepiece of the garden, its sheet of water edged with stone and set in mown grass to counterpoint the rich planting in the deep mixed borders on either side. In the pool itself the planting is limited, and any more would upset the architectural symmetry, but four large terracotta pots on the stone-flagged corners of the pool complete the design to perfection.

LEFT Fragrant lilies, including *L.* 'Casa Blanca' and *L.* 'Stargazer', provide a welcome at the entrance to Great Dixter. Benefiting from the sheltered site and contributing to the sub-tropical look are *Pseudopanax lessonii* 'Gold Splash', several begonias and the fleshy star of an agave.

RIGHT The planting in this striking pot – just a simple posy of pansies – is deliberately restrained so as not to detract from the pot's architectural purpose as the centrepiece of a metal arbour.

Whether in spring, before the borders come to life, or at the height of summer, with their complementary hot and pale schemes (see pages 38-41), the four terracotta pots link the pool garden's planting and architecture without either repeating the style of the former or intruding into the qualities of the latter.

The twice-yearly planting of the pool garden pots at Tintinhull reflects the classic succession from spring to summer in garden borders, but pot-life can have other rhythms. At Great Dixter the colonies of pots, each with its own plant variety, undergo a system of constant rotation that is refreshing, but only easily achieved so long as the supply of new plants from potting shed, greenhouse or cold frame is guaranteed. In contrast, Rosemary Verey plans for her larger pots to provide their own succession. They are replanted twice a year, in October and May. Through the winter, a central evergreen such as clipped box, holly or the variegated sea buckthorn, *Rhamnus alaternus* 'Argenteovariegata' will provide constant shape. Around them are planted tulips (a single variety in each pot) planted lowest, then a layer of compost with narcissi placed above, sometimes hyacinths above these and with species *Crocus chrysanthus* on top. Mixed with the crocuses are 'Paper White' narcissi; these flower first, often around Christmas. The crocuses are in flower in February and the tulips will continue into May. Planting so many bulbs in layers like this may seem to make a pot very crowded but, as Rosemary Verey reassures, 'remember they will always push their way up through each other.'

Where spring bulbs are limited to single varieties in each pot or tub, the summer-flowering combinations at Barnsley are planned for harmonious blends to be suitable for their allotted position and, without the evergreen centrepiece, are free to intermingle. In the courtyard tubs, ivy and scented-leaved geraniums are mixed with silver helichrysum; a well-tried, classic grouping that exactly serves its purpose, to bring summer up to the very edge of the house. On the veranda the plant combination is chosen to complement the honey-coloured Cotswold stone of the house wall: 'The yellow daisy-flowered *Bidens ferulifolia* clambers through *Helichrysum petiolare*, surrounding golden variegated box;

The pots are planted seasonally twice a year, the simplicity of tulips in spring to harmonize with the predominantly architectural mood of the garden at this time of year giving way to rich summer mixtures to complement the borders in full flower around the garden's perimeters. Penelope Hobhouse describes a typical planting: 'Our summer schemes vary but are similar each year, with plants grown from cuttings and seed. For several years we used centrally placed *Argyranthemum foeniculaceum*, with glaucous leaves and white daisy flowers, surrounded by a mixture of pink nemesias, the little mallow-like *Hibiscus trionum*, with cream maroon-centred flowers, silver helichrysums, and trailing verbenas – both dark blue 'Hidcote Purple' and 'Silver Anne', a pale pink. In the past we have had red-flowered flax (*Linum grandiflorum* 'Rubrum'). *Anisodontea* × *hypomadara*, from South Africa, is another good centrepiece.'

LEFT The wooden half barrels in Rosemary Verey's courtyard garden see a succession of spring planting. This combination of narcissi and tulips is the high point after the weeks of crocuses and smaller early bulbs.

RIGHT *Clematis florida* 'Sieboldii', with its passionflower-like blooms, makes a superb partner for *Fuchsia* 'Chequerboard', its twining stems also adding a sense of movement.

combinations that are long-lasting and satisfying.' As containers often have a house wall as a backdrop, it is worth thinking about suitable contrasts and harmonies. Against the whitewashed interior of the classical temple, Rosemary Verey chooses a quite different planting: 'In summer several of our specimen pelargoniums show up well against the whitewashed walls.' In most years the pelargoniums here are limited to varieties in a single colour such as pink or pale mauve, as she has found that a mixture of colours against the bright white background is not successful.

These are Rosemary Verey's regular combinations for pots, easy to assemble and guaranteed to perform each year, but she also finds containers invaluable for protecting and displaying treasures and rarities. Auriculas require attention and are often unsatisfactory when grown as a border plant but massed together in a tub they can be nurtured to display their tapestry of velvety colours. Tender salvias that might not compete with more boisterous neighbours in a border thrive on being grown alone in pots and are moved inside at the end of autumn for winter protection. Hostas, especially those with really luxuriant leaves such as *Hosta sieboldiana*, have a regularity of shape that is ideally suited to massing in a tub positioned in a shady corner and are far more easily protected against slugs than is often possible when they are out in the garden.

How often gardeners face the situation of not having suitable soil or aspect to grow an especially favoured plant. Invariably they are not worth struggling with in these circumstances, invalids surrounded by healthy neighbours. But their particular needs can be easily accommodated in a container, the right soil mixture brought in to suit their requirements. If you do not have the cool, woody and neutral to acid soil required by camellias, the conditions can be created in a large tub. Sculptural, architectural evergreens that

add year-round shape to so many gardens, few shrubs are so well suited to container growing as camellias. Except in parts of the country where they can attain generous size camellias can look out of place in the traditional woodland setting, and are better grown as formal specimens for the neatness of their habit.

Another shrub that benefits from the conditions and attention available when grown in containers is the hydrangea, especially those with blue-shaded domes of flowers that, faded into parchment brown in late autumn, will stay through to spring. Penelope Hobhouse, while considering them as naturally woodland plants, extols the architectural qualities that, like those of camellias, make them perfect for container growing: 'A pair can frame a gateway or define a vista or a single specimen can be treated as a focal point … I have to say that I covet the incredibly vivid wash of blue

LEFT When chosen for its strong outline, a single plant in a container can provide an impressively architectural statement in an area of mixed planting. This *Cordyline australis* 'Torbay Dazzler' is perfectly placed to light up this vine-hung corner.

RIGHT Here, at the Manor House, Heslington, containers are used for primarily architectural purpose, flanking either side of the doorway from garden to house. The 'sentinel' role is emphasized by the clipped box's immaculate spirals.

produced by mop-headed hortensia hydrangeas growing in rich acidic soil … In limey soil the colour of the sterile florets becomes a muddy bluish-pink. If, like me, you garden on neutral or alkaline soil, it is well worth considering growing the blue forms in containers with a specially prepared mix of acidic soil, or soil that has been treated with a blueing compound of aluminium sulphate.'

Both hydrangeas and camellias are plants whose architectural potential makes them ideal for containers. This principle of using plants that do not always immediately suggest themselves for container growing is endlessly applicable. At Sticky Wicket Pam Lewis shows two interesting and totally contrasting examples in pots on the house's narrow north-facing terrace. In one she grows the *Kirengeshoma palmata* that Beth Chatto so admires and grows in a damp, shady bed near her water garden (see page 63). At Sticky Wicket the lime-free, woody soil in which the plant thrives is not available, but can be supplied in a pot; the north-facing aspect provides a good degree of shade. Grown in such a manner, the fine details of the maple-like foliage and butter yellow flowers can be enjoyed at close quarters. In the other pot, to maintain colour continuity, she grows pale lemon-flowered *Coreopsis verticiliata* 'Moonbeam', an outstanding late-summer border plant, but one whose intensity of flower and bushy habit are ideally shown off in a container.

Penelope Hobhouse and Pam Lewis both reveal in their plantings how, regardless of what you wish to grow, the right preparation is an essential ingredient of successful container gardening. Drainage combined with sufficient moisture and nutrients are essential, as are position in sun or shade depending on your chosen plants' requirements. For Pam Lewis it is a simple equation: 'big pots, plus few plants of few varieties, good compost plus a feed mid-season and dead-heading continuously, equals a big result.'

Pam Lewis's single-minded preferences about her containers emphasize that, to a greater degree that any other part of the garden, containers offer the potential to be what you want them to be. Today, this is an indispensable part of their role. In a small town garden, where the preference is for architectural foliage

plants, a tub filled with luxuriant white lilies is all you need to introduce a note of flowering richness. Containers can offer solutions, enable you to grow things that would struggle elsewhere in your garden, and provide continuity in a number of ways –

between seasons, between different areas, between house and garden and the garden's larger character. In the end, this idea of continuity is significant because, as Paul Williams suggests, containers should always be chosen, positioned and planted as part of the garden, not as a bolt-on. For, as he says, 'In the end, the principles of design and plant combinations are exactly the same for both container and border.' Such a combination is, perhaps, the essence of classic planting.

CONTEMPORARY PLANTING

'Nowadays we are trying hard to return to nature, perhaps because we are overcivilized. Also, many people travel and have the opportunity to see plants growing in their natural habitat. Some may feel the urge to try and cultivate these plants seen growing in the wild to bring something of the peace and tranquillity of nature into their own gardens.'

BETH CHATTO

Mixing the traditional and the unusual in carefully thought-out plant associations is a feature of contemporary planting. At Eastgrove Cottage the metallic-hued leaves of *Rosa glauca* are teamed, not with predictable pinks and mauves, but with the more arresting pale yellow combination of *Kniphofia* 'Sunningdale Yellow', *Tanacetum parthenium* 'Aureum' and *Anthemis tinctoria* 'E.C. Buxton'.

LEFT In Beth Chatto's garden the planting merges without break from waterside to woodland beyond. Foxglove spires dot the planting as they would do in a natural woodland setting, and honeysuckles (*Lonicera periclymenum*) cascade from a tree behind. Also flourishing in this semi-wilderness are *Hosta sieboldiana elegans*, hydrangeas and an elder with heavily spotted leaves, *Sambucus nigra* 'Pulverulenta'.

RIGHT The shapes of grasses, euphorbias and sun-loving alliums (especially when they have gone to seed like these *A. cristophii*), contrasted here with wine-coloured *Penstemon* 'Andenken an Friedrich Hahn', are indispensable to the concept of a gravel garden.

There are a number of leading contemporary gardeners who have brought about a revolution in the concept of planting and none more so than Beth Chatto. In the past, whatever planting a border contained, the ideas behind its conditions and management derived from a series of widely accepted principles. A border was, by definition, a formally shaped feature with the soil and other growing conditions often artificially changed from their natural state to enable you to garden along the accepted lines. Now, however, the sense of regulation has been released and a border can just as easily be a 'natural habitat for suitable groups of plants, within a garden setting'.

Beth Chatto has been at the forefront of this change in emphasis. Her successes, irrefutably classic, that are now so widely admired, derive from the simple desire to familiarize herself with the natural conditions of an area within her garden, and to choose and grow a selection of plants for which those conditions are as ideal as possible. Her Essex garden is possibly in one of the most demanding situations in England for traditional gardening: much of the soil is poor and thin over sand and gravel; rainfall is rarely over 50 cm (20 in) a year and summer drought the norm rather than an occasional hazard; winter cold and winds can be extreme.

Her aim to plant harmoniously with the natural conditions, be they dry or damp, has led to a vital change in planting that is especially noticeable in summer. Instead of flowering display being the primary aim, the plants throughout her garden are grown and grouped as much, or more, for their shape and overall form. Flowers and foliage together produce, in her own words, 'a plant landscape', a synthesis of the garden and nature. But while firm on certain principles of planting she is equally firm that personal choice should have a say. 'The way you group plants together is the whole essence of gardening. There are many ways of doing this – which is just as it should be – it would be very dull if everybody put their plants together in the same way. Designing a garden is rather like painting. Two painters will take the same pigments and will produce an entirely different picture, just as we do with our plants.'

The most fundamental of her ground rules for the garden is that plants should be suitable for the basic conditions. This philosophy is inspired by her belief in the intrinsic bond between plants in nature and plants in a garden, a belief originally encouraged by her husband's researches as a plant ecologist. This bond is so simple as to be often overlooked, she says, especially by gardening beginners. 'Many gardeners are not aware that the most well known garden plants have been developed by hybridization and selection from plants found growing in the wild. They tend to

think of them as products of the horticulturist.' Seeing and admiring certain plants growing in certain conditions in the wild, and the companion plants they naturally associated with, instilled in Beth Chatto a determination that the planning of her garden would be guided by these observations.

The long border at the entrance to her garden is free-draining, gravelly soil and through the summer its moisture content will be minimal – sometimes non-existent. She describes the plants that thrive here: 'They have all been chosen because they can withstand these conditions, with leathery leaves (like bergenias), or finely cut leaves (like santolinas) or fat leaves (like sedums) to help them to retain moisture.' Planting in groups rather than a collection of individual specimens originally helped inject the necessary scale to the planting here, as the entrance border has impressive proportions – some 300 m long and over 6 m deep (975×20 ft) – and is, with a backing hedge of × *Cupressocyparis leylandii*, the most formally shaped area she has created. But where it typifies the planting style that predominates everywhere else in her garden is the recognizable manner in which plants are included and associated first and foremost for shape. The bergenias have expanded into extensive colonies, with their great plate-like leaves present, slowly changing their hue, through most of the year. *Sedum* 'Herbstfreude', similarly long-seasoned, provides hummocks of fleshy leaves and stems, a complete contrast to the bristling silvery candelabra of *Eryngium giganteum*, another major character that has self-seeded itself about the border. This highly ornamental thistle associates with a number of different neighbours: with clumps of the flattened yellow flowers of achillea, next to fuzzy club heads of euphorbias, or in front of verbascums (mulleins), whose furry grey spires punctuate the planting. The mulleins are one of a selection of bold statements that add scale and body to the planting, others are cardoons (*Cynara cardunculus*) and sprays of the giant feather grass, *Stipa gigantea*.

This underlying priority of form is what binds the planting together so successfully and gives it such an appearance of permanence. Individual plants make their own statement as well

The gravel in Beth Chatto's gravel garden forms a dry river bed along whose banks the plant colonies link up their different shapes and forms, supplemented by islands of flower colour as the season progresses.

as playing their part in relation to their immediate neighbours, and to less closely associated groups, so that low domes contrast with striking verticals, fleshy stems with feathery fronds, shiny leaves with hairy. The high proportion of grey or silver foliage – partly practical, because such plants are better equipped to thrive in the dry conditions – gives a harmonious but varied colour palette against which the changing tones and highlights of flower colour interact.

The entrance borders are just one of the areas of Beth Chatto's garden where poor soil and little moisture retention combine. There are, however, two areas where her gardening philosophy has become most celebrated – the Mediterranean or dry garden, and the more recent gravel garden, created since 1991. In these, the controlling influence is dryness, and a comparison between the two areas shows how Beth Chatto's approach to planting has developed over the years.

The dry garden is definitely a garden, a man-made habitat close to the house, in a series of raised beds that have changed and been improved over the years. Different mixtures of leaf mould, compost and grit have been added to the soil, although the underlying dryness remains. The majority of the plants here all thrive in the conditions provided – many originate from lands around the Mediterranean where their natural habitat is similar – and they have proved extremely resilient. They do not pop up and die down in the way that many hybridized border perennials accustomed to a richer diet do. This advantage, coupled with the emphasis on foliage, a more important characteristic with many than their flowers, means that there is shape and colour in the dry garden through much of the year. Again, silver-leaved plants are plentiful: domes of artemisias and santolinas beside rosettes of young verbascums or contrasting with the greens and yellows of different euphorbias; the silvery blue stems of pinks (*Dianthus*) offsetting their bright, sweet-scented flowers. Many of the flowers are brilliantly coloured – pink, orange, white or yellow predominate – but they have a small-scale, fleeting habit, which Beth Chatto knows is entirely suitable for the style of planting, and for

single stems. These taller stems also play a vital role in the plant grouping, which Beth Chatto describes as an asymmetrical triangle. 'Looking at it in profile, we pass through tiny-leaved, sweetly scented thymes, and groups of low-gowing euphorbias, through larger mounds of silvery grey lavender and *Ballota*, to *Euphorbia wulfenii*, which is taller still, until we meet a little Judas tree (*Cercis siliquastrum*), which is not very tall yet. But the eye has been lifted as the line leads up to the sky, to the *Cupressus arizonica* beyond, a useful drought-loving coniferous tree. The skyline does not look as though the plants have been pushed in like walking sticks in a hatstand.'

To move from the dry garden to the gravel garden is to advance in concept to the gardening frontier. For this is a plant landscape, a human creation, but taking not only its inspiration but its form and design directly from nature. The fact that it was previously the car park for visitors to Beth Chatto's garden and nursery is coincidental, but it seems to emphasize the element of 'nature reclaiming its own' in this new garden. In describing how she designed the garden Beth Chatto shows its landscape inspiration. 'I had in mind a dried-up river bed winding between shallow banks and islands, so using every available hosepipe, I laid out the wide central path to curve gently between mixed borders and the occasional island bed.' The path is shingle and while the original gravelly, sandy soil was initially enhanced with compost the plants all grow out of gravel. In a manner that recalls Japanese gardens the result is both an allegory and a real picture.

The plants are all intrinsically drought resistant because the fundamental maintenance limitation of the gravel garden is that it should not be watered. In a manner that you would normally have to travel to the Mediterranean, parts of North America or

her it gives an impression of a pointilliste painting: 'Most of the flowers appear as vivid dots of colour against a background of predominantly grey foliage.'

Perhaps most relevant in comparison to a traditional border are the two issues of overall structure and the proportion of foliage to flowers. Unlike a traditional border, there is no sense of the planting having a 'sense of direction' or an over-riding repeated rhythm. Instead, the plants themselves dictate the composition, and the semi-permanent foliage serves as a background medium on to which flower colour appears in a painterly manner.

Because many of the plants have a dense or bushy habit the vertical contrasts are a vital ingredient and many of those chosen by Beth Chatto exaggerate their upward movement with slender elegance: crêpe-paper poppies; the wand-like, white-flowered *Gaura lindheimeri*; alliums with drumstick flower heads in varying sizes and shades of purple and their cousin, *Nectaroscordum siculum bulgaricum*, with its greeny plum-flushed flowers drooping off tall

LEFT A modernist plant combination, in which a sculptural agave is surrounded by low clumps of verbenas, gazanias and *Anthemis cretica*.

RIGHT Beth Chatto's 'jewel box': in her gravel garden the overriding impression of the planting is of a lightness of colour and form that would be found in a natural, untended plant landscape.

South Africa to see, the plants give the impression of defying the harsh conditions but this is an illusion and the garden's achievement is that they revel in them because they are closely comparable to their natural habitat. It is difficult to pinpoint why the gravel garden has such a radically different atmosphere from more conventional plant groupings in borders, but it has something to do

focal point.' This is largely because, 'plants grown in gravel soils tend to be tough and wiry rather than soft and lush while the land itself is drier and warmer in winter than heavy clay soils.'

The gravel garden is protected from the north-east winds that are the winter curse of the Essex coast by the same leylandii hedge that continues on from behind the entrance borders. And

LEFT Plant shapes are as important in the contemporary garden as flower colour.

RIGHT In growing up beside a tuft of squirrel-tail grass, *Hordeum jubatum*, a self-seeded pansy has provided an unintentional but highly successful juxtaposition of velvety petals and soft, hairy ears of grass.

with the sense of movement instilled by the flowing paths of shingle and their harmonious merging without break into the foliage of plants. Another factor is the way many of the individual plants combine seemingly ephemeral fragility with light but dazzling brilliance. The shapes are complemented by this patchwork of colour which Beth Chatto likens to a jewel box. The effect is achieved because she uses species plants with relatively small or simple flowers. 'They can be used more daringly than one would care to risk with blocks of bedding plants, while their flowering time extends from early spring to late autumn,' she explains. 'In winter good structure remains, a warm living palette of foliage, seedheads and grasses while the pale sweep of gravel becomes the

while the planting contains many verticals among the interlinking groups of lower-growing plants, few of them are blocky. These factors combine with the open aspect to bring about an unusual variety of sunlight effects which Beth Chatto has picked up on with the planting. There is no real 'front' or 'back' in the gravel garden, plant shapes and forms do not graduate from low to tall but move far more freely, and the quantities of perennial grasses, as well as tall plants of spidery habit such as *Verbena bonariensis*, create an upper haze of foliage through which the light plays on to their surrounding neighbours.

The perennial grasses are intrinsic to the overall planting effect. Not only are they present for much of the year, especially coming

RIGHT Yellow and blue form a pleasing and classic combination, beautifully illustrated by these achilleas among the contrasting forms and shades of violas, salvias and delphiniums.

into their own in that 'difficult' time, from autumn through winter, but more than anything else in the gravel garden they instil an atmosphere of naturalism. With the gravel they are the background canvas on to which the greys and greens and white, the quantities of yellow, and the seasonal flashes of pink, orange and magenta, are all painted.

Many of the plants most evident in the gravel garden are both common and – to many gardeners – extremely ordinary. But to plants in the wild their survival is more about being healthy than being rare and showy. There are rarities here – at least in British gardens – such as unusual lavenders or *Phlomis tuberosa* 'Amazone', but over and above any individual qualities the gravel garden seeks to merge garden and nature in a manner that for many people looks to the future of our gardens. When we are not allowed to water from year to year and dry summers extend into dry autumns, there will be an increasing interest in drought-resistant plants and those from traditionally warmer climates that come into their own after weeks of heat. The fascinating equation is how the spartan, minimalist maintenance regime produces a picture of such richly varied brilliance. The primary ingredient is the plantsmanship behind the choice and arrangement which, while achieving an untraditional effect, does so with adherence to strong principles.

Beth Chatto has always been in the vanguard of such a contemporary style of planting, but its application is ever-widening, whether in the United States in the work of leading designers and plantsmen Wolfgang Oehme and James van Sweden, in the sweeping drifts of park gardens in Germany, or in the concentration on colonies of indigenous plants in South African gardens. And certainly, such principles are similarly valued by Pam Lewis in her Dorset garden, Sticky Wicket. As she said about plants for a border, 'Don't worry about what they are and what their names

are, or whether you are going to fit in your favourites; look at the plants for shape, character and shades and whether they're happy with what they're growing with, and that makes combinations much easier.'

As the garden's name suggests, the site is on heavy, sticky clay, and because Pam Lewis has also chosen plants particularly suited to her conditions, the range is very different from Beth Chatto's. The plants are also chosen to harmonize with Pam Lewis's gardening philosophy: 'Our ambition is to create an ecological haven, using the land productively, keeping in balance with nature and enhancing our immediate environment rather than intruding upon it. Our garden is designed more for artist and naturalist than

those seeking botanical or horticultural excellence. It is where we study and demonstrate the 'art of planting', experimenting with associations of colour, form and texture of foliage and flower.'

Pam Lewis's ideas on the 'art of planting' have encouraged her to develop a technique similar to the colour swatches of interior decorators or fabric makers. She cuts out pages of plant catalogues and pastes together compatible plants with complementary colours to create a sheet of different shades. In its painterly concept it looks back to Gertrude Jekyll's ideas on colour as set out in her book *Colour Schemes for the Flower Garden*. But at Sticky Wicket its application is contemporary, using Pam Lewis's favourite plants, often grouped in large quantities, with others integrated between. This and the broad philosophy of the planting is exemplified in the round garden, which forms the garden's hub and focus on one side of the house. The borders in the round garden are designed as a series of segments to make up the whole picture, and Pam Lewis combines them for their colours in a progression of shades from pale cream through pinks and mauves to deep magenta and red. Many plants she uses are familiar and often used repetitively to create a living palette. In summer, when the colour shade effect is at its height, the result is sensational. The combinations are natural and yet striking – alliums growing out

many well-known and reliable plants. As Pam Lewis comments, 'there are lots of cottage garden favourites such as aquilegia, iris, lupins, foxgloves, campanulas, and phlox … we have a rich selection of hardy geraniums, their shades of pink, mauve, blue and white, enhancing the gentle flow of colours in the borders.'

There are also many types of plants that are less widely grown but, like Beth Chatto's choice of Mediterranean perennials, all are notably self-reliant. The airiness that Beth Chatto has introduced

LEFT The flowing lines of the round garden at Sticky Wicket encourage the sense of movement through the colours of adjoining beds and areas. It is easy to see how the repetition of certain plants - notably easy-to-grow perennials such as hardy geraniums, sages, thymes and catmint (*Nepeta*) – provides an understated framework to the planting.

RIGHT As poppies lose their petals their seedheads make a quite different but equally interesting contribution to the summer garden, especially at the beginning or end of the day, when their hard round seed cases are caught by the low sun.

of a silvery blue haze of *Eryngium* 'Calypso' or dark purple and pink knautias massed together.

In many of the round garden's beds shrub roses and buddlejas give structure to the perennial plants. It is a classic combination and yet here, the subtle variations in style, the overall design and colour movements contribute to a highly original effect. Perhaps this is the main quality of the garden, the inspired combinations of

by her colonies of waving grasses is also an important element of Sticky Wicket, but provided here by quite different plants, in particular scabious types such as the knautias, astrantias and creamy cephalarias, which suit the open sunny aspect where they can be seen in silhouette to show off their delicate form.

The planting is the pre-eminent feature of Pam Lewis's round garden and, as in Beth Chatto's garden, it is the achievement of an overall, harmonious picture, always lively, sometimes vibrant, that enhances the individual forms and colours. At the same time there is a conscious design, created by the dissecting paths which as Pam Lewis says, 'give a formal structure to the informal planting'.

Contemporary planters are as aware of the relationship between formal and informal as any of their predecessors, conscious of its engrained existence on the gardening psyche. But, as Penelope Hobhouse explains about her new garden at Bettiscombe in Dorset, when the combinations are right the distinctions between formal and informal that are so often suspected of dividing gardening styles, are merged by the style of planting. Indeed she goes so far as to say her preference is for 'jungles; inside a strong structured shape.'

The garden at Bettiscombe draws on Penelope Hobhouse's immense experience of gardening and planting in different situations around the world. But this treasury of knowledge is given freedom by the fact that here Penelope Hobhouse is gardening for herself and her aspirations are as clearly contemporary and forward-looking as those of both Beth Chatto and Pam Lewis. The house, a converted coach house, squarely separates the garden's two areas, on one side open and merging into the landscape of Dorset hills beyond, on the other a secret square enclosed by high walls. Originally this area sloped but was converted into two levels, the smaller, upper one overlooking the other from one side. Penelope Hobhouse says that 'planting throughout the garden has been designed to make less work in the years to come to ease my gardening old age' but such practical considerations are only an encouragement for the planting style that she wished to create.

Throughout the walled garden there is a sense of structural plants providing the framework for seasonal colour and form. On the upper terrace it is strongly provided by an avenue of globe locust trees, *Robinia pseudoacacia* 'Umbraculifera', and pillars of *Phillyrea latifolia*, as well as metal arches for rambling roses and late-flowering clematis that span the central path. To this framework

have been added climbers and wall shrubs as a backcloth – all now intertwined: ceanothus and clematis, a white Banksian rose, climbing hydrangeas and different solanums, both purple and white. Within the structure of these plants a medley of perennials interrelate through the summer – hardy geraniums and hollyhocks (*Alcea rosea*), polemoniums and alchemilla with the more exotic shapes of bronze fennel and showering *Crambe cordifolia*. These classic and well-loved plants are given a new twist by the comparative quantities in which they are planted, the preponderance of structural plants exaggerating the prolific nature of the smaller intermingled perennials.

The main area of the walled garden was transformed in 1995 by the replacement of the central rectangle of lawn with gravel, not least because of Penelope Hobhouse's admiration for Beth Chatto's gravel garden. The pillars of yew (mirroring those on the other side of the house) and the yew hedges that back them on either side were retained, but the garden's character would be transformed by the new priority. 'I wanted to create a gravel garden in which some shrubs would give structure around the existing yews, but where the rest of the planting would be of Mediterranean-type plants, many of which would self-seed and form spreading naturalistic groups.'

Even now, only a short time after the garden was begun, this is already a plant landscape; small-scale but of wonderfully bold form and shapes into which colour interplays without ever dominating. The shrubs include shiny-leaved elaeagnus and a variety of olearias but the shapes of perennials are equally prominent: thistly onopordums, eryngiums, echinops and *Galactites tomentosa*; lime green towers of euphorbias; spires of self-seeding *Salvia* 'Indigo Spires' and groups of the similarly upward-reaching *Perovskia atriplicifolia*, *Sisyrinchium striatum* and various nicotianas. Intermittent colour splashes come from poppies and yellow *Glaucium flavum*. The way the plants are grouped together, some growing visibly out of the gravel base, others so closely merged that the gravel is obscured, provide a sense of enormous vigour that seems to need the constant cool green clipped yew for containment. It

The low plant landscape at Sticky Wicket gives the appearance of constantly moving froth in this mixture of allium seedheads among *Artemisia alba* 'Canescens', *Agrostis nebulosa* and violas raised by Pam Lewis.

is exactly the idea of 'jungles with a structure' that she has been seeking to attain.

The garden at Bettiscombe will continue to evolve. The outer orchard on either side of the central mown yew avenue is still very young, and the newly planted mulberry trees and crab apples will change the whole character of this part of the garden as they mature. The meadow grass into which the fruit trees have been planted is dotted with spring bulbs, and here the plant colony will always require attention in the spring and high summer and enable Penelope Hobhouse to experiment with her gardening ideas. At times she feels the garden may end up almost exclusively broad-leaved evergreen shrubs and in shades of green and silver foliage with small-flowered late summer clematis. But this extreme is perhaps unlikely: 'Bettiscombe has given me a chance

to design for myself, with strong structured outlines, but also to return to my original passion for plants. I believe it is possible to combine classic principles with the collector's urge to have a very wide selection.'

The lure of a gardening jungle, the collector's urge to move on to growing new plants, a pioneering appreciation that bold shapes and colour are classic ingredients of contemporary planting, and a humorous enjoyment of the debate about gardening taste – all played their part in Christopher Lloyd's transformation a few years ago of the rose garden at Great Dixter. He described removing the roses as getting rid of friends of fifty years' standing but, as he wrote about the revolution (carried out with the help and encouragement of his friend and head gardener, Fergus Garrett), 'What would suit a formally designed garden of this kind, other

ABOVE Bold plant associations are entirely contemporary and no one has given them more impetus than Christopher Lloyd at Great Dixter: dark dahlias, cannas, *Verbena bonariensis* and *Cyperus papyrus* are among the plants that have replaced the shrub roses that once grew here.

RIGHT The long border is in a sense the planting heart of the garden at Great Dixter, its associations as effective when seen here in close detail as when making up part of the overall picture.

than roses? … The site is very sheltered and very hot in summer. Last year, we tried plugging the gaps left by defunct roses with cannas – an elegant, easy and prolific one, *Canna indica* 'Purpurea'. It has narrow, purplish leaves, an upright habit to six or seven feet and small red flowers in considerable abundance. It revelled in the rose garden and was particularly striking with a margin between it and the paths of self-sown, purple-flowered *Verbena bonariensis*.' Now, some years after the inception of the new garden, it is intriguing to see what Christopher Lloyd said at the time and how accurately his ideas have turned to fruition.

'What we shall therefore now aim for is a summer garden of voluptuous luxuriance. The garden is cut off from other areas, so you will suddenly and unexpectedly be plunged into it. As you fight your way through an overhanging jungle on either side, your progress may sometimes be entirely blocked. But there are plenty of paths and alternative routes, so you can try again along one of these. There'll be no planting plan and I have as yet unformulated ideas of what will be included, aside from cannas, the verbena, castor oil plants (*Ricinus*), perhaps dahlias, *Melianthus major*.'

All these plants he envisaged are there, together with others, contributing to the exotic atmosphere of his 'summer garden of

ABOVE Bold contrasts: the scarlet of *Salvia coccinea* 'Lady in Red' vibrates against the graceful grass, *Elymus magellanicus*.

LEFT Although as airy as thistledown, the great lollipop-like heads of *Allium cristophii* make an impression whether in flower or gone to seed.

FAR RIGHT This unconventional group of potted plants makes a stunning temporary display: the clashing colours of *Begonia sutherlandii* and magenta petunias are brought together by the bright-painted coleus leaves, their hot tones cooled by the silver rosettes of a cotyledon.

voluptuous luxuriance'. No part of Great Dixter is left to be truly self-sufficient but this garden has become a plant landscape of shapes and textures as well as brilliant colours, within a framework. The luxuriance disguises the selection and choice involved in securing the strong effect of bright reds, oranges and yellows against enormous fronds of green foliage, without which the garden would be chaotic. Single or group themes are repeated rather than a host of characters being mixed together and, as all the gardens in this and other chapters demonstrate, this enables their creators to produce quite different but equally lasting effects from a huge range of the plant spectrum.

Great Dixter also emphasizes the point that, even in the most old-established of settings, contemporary planting can be adventurous without jarring. Whether it is for a specific new area such as this, or for a whole garden, the plants dictate both the detail and the overall appearance, and in the scene created the importance of colour is at least equalled by the considerations of shape and texture.

ACKNOWLEDGEMENTS

Classic Planting relies heavily on the distinguished group of gardeners on whose work the text and illustrations focus and my principal debt of thanks – reiterated below by Tony Lord – is to them: Louisa Arbuthnott, Lord Ashbrook, Jim and Sarah Buckland, Beth Chatto, Fergus Garrett, Penelope Hobhouse, Sibylle Kreutzberger, Pam Lewis, Christopher Lloyd, Monique Paice, Nori and Sandra Pope, Pam Schwerdt, Carol and Malcolm Skinner, Rosemary Verey and Paul Williams. The book would not come alive without the photographs for which I must primarily thank Tony Lord. It has been a thoroughly enjoyable partnership, although the visits we did together were plagued by torrential rain. I must also thank the select group of other leading garden photographers who made their work available for the book.

As well as quotes from comments that the group of gardeners made to me, there are a number of quotations from published works and I am extremely grateful to the following publishers. Frances Lincoln: Rosemary Verey's *Making of a Garden*, and Penelope Hobhouse's *On Gardening*; Harper Collins: Beth Chatto's *The Green Tapestry*, and Russell Page's *The Education of a Gardener*; Bloomsbury: Christopher Lloyd's *In My Garden*; Robin Lane Fox: Robin Lane Fox's *Better Gardening*.

Emily van Eesteren at Cassell first suggested the book and I must thank her not only for that but for seeing through a production schedule that was occasionally testing due to my being overseas. Similarly involved at that stage as editor was Caroline Ball, whose cheerful efficiency and attention to detail pulled the book together. I must also thank Clare Churly and Alison Goff at Cassell, my agent Vivienne Schuster and, not least, as my dedication suggests – my wife Rara for the combination of encouragement and tolerance that writers' spouses need to develop.

GEORGE PLUMPTRE

PHOTOGRAPHIC ACKNOWLEDGEMENTS

It has been a great pleasure to visit such marvellous gardens to assemble photographs for this book. Most of my pictures were taken in 1997, with a few taken in earlier years, using a Canon T90 camera and Fuji Velvia 35mm film. At every garden I received the utmost hospitality and co-operation from owners and head gardeners, all of whom allowed me to visit at unearthly and doubtless inconvenient times. To all of the following I owe my grateful thanks: at Arley Hall, Lord Ashbrook and head gardener Paul Cook; at Barnsley, Rosemary Verey; at Beth Chatto Gardens, Beth Chatto; at Bourton House, Monique Paice and head gardener Paul Williams; at Birlingham Manor, Jane Williams-Thomas; at Eastgrove Cottage, Carol and Malcolm Skinner; at Great Dixter, Christopher Lloyd and head gardener Fergus Garrett; Pam Schwerdt and Sibylle Kreutzberger; at Manor House, Heslington, George Smith; at Hill Bark, Malcolm Simm and Tim Gittins; at Hadspen, Nori and Sandra Pope; at The Menagerie, head gardener Penny Hammond; at Stone House Cottage, James and Louisa Arbuthnott; at Sticky Wicket, Pam Lewis; at West Dean, Jim and Sarah Buckland.

TONY LORD

All photographs by Tony Lord except the following:
Jerry Harpur 45, 92 (Tintinhull Garden, Somerset), 114 right, 117 right, 125 (Helmingham Hall, Suffolk); **Marcus Harpur** 67; **Anne Hyde** front cover (Sue Hillwood-Harris, 133 Crystal Palace Road, London SE22), 14–15 (Mr J. Drake, Hardwicke House, Fen Ditton, Cambs), 53 (Clapton Court, Somerset), 66 (Sir Edward and Lady Tomkins, Winslow Hall, Winslow, Bucks), 132 (Michael Goulding Esq., Hipkins, Broxbourne, Herts), 148 right (Mr and Mrs N. Coote, 40 Osler Rd, Headington, Oxford); **Andrew Lawson** 16, 40 (Tintinhull Garden, Somerset), 41 (Tintinhull Gardens, Somerset), 54 (Hadspen Gardens, Somerset), 63, 75, 78 right (Gothic House, Oxfordshire), 86 (Tintinhull Garden, Somerset), 87, 91 (Tintinhull Garden, Somerset), 116, 147 (Beth Chatto Gardens, Essex), 149 (Sticky Wicket, Buckland Newton, Dorset), 150 (Sticky Wicket, Buckland Newton, Dorset); **Clive Nichols** 12–13, 17, 26, 28 (Barnsley House, Gloucestershire), 32, 70–71 (Cambridge Botanic Garden), 76–77 (The Old Vicarage, Norfolk), 78 left, 79 right, 80, 81 (Cambridge Winter Garden), 85 left (Beth Chatto Gardens, Essex), 102 (Brook Cottage, Oxfordshire), 108 above (Barnsley House, Gloucestershire), 110 (Tintinhull Garden, Somerset), 115 (Barnsley House, Gloucestershire), 120 (Bourton House, Gloucestershire), 126–127 (Beth Chatto Gardens, Essex), 131 (Sticky Wicket, Buckland Newton, Dorset), 133 (Beth Chatto Gardens, Essex), 136 (Barnsley House, Gloucestershire), 146 (Beth Chatto Gardens, Essex).

INDEX